Ernst & Young Entrepreneur of the Year Case Series

Ernst & Young Entrepreneur of the Year Case Series

EDITED BY
COLETTE HENRY

This book was typeset by ARK Imaging for

BLACKHALL PUBLISHING
33 Carysfort Avenue
Blackrock
Co. Dublin
Ireland

e-mail: info@blackhallpublishing.com
www.blackhallpublishing.com

ISBN: 978-1-84218-141-6

A catalogue record for this book is available from the British Library.

Printed in Ireland by Betaprint

Foreword

Life as an entrepreneur can be exciting and all consuming. Entrepreneurs imbue in those around them a 'can do' attitude. They pursue their dreams, both large and small, and strive to turn them into reality.

Entrepreneurs who set up a new venture employing ten people are as much of a success story as those who set up a business employing 200. Small businesses are the backbone of the Irish economy.

There has never been a better time to break out and set up a new venture. Right now we have the perfect storm – a high growth economy, low inflation, growing disposable income, a country full of confidence and people looking to invest in entrepreneurship.

The entrepreneurial stories in this collection of case studies are fascinating. They provide an insight into how ideas for a new venture are conceived, how they are spawned and then burst to life. Everybody can learn from these stories.

The companies in the following case studies ought to be saluted for their generosity in helping to create the next wave of Irish entrepreneurs. No one entrepreneur can say they have it all in terms of knowledge. We all learn from one another's setbacks, challenges and successes.

When you have finished reading these case studies and you want to start your own venture, don't wait, don't hold back, get going immediately. And remember, in entrepreneurship you make your own luck!

Denis O'Brien
Chairman
Digicel

ERNST & YOUNG
ENTREPRENEUR
OF THE YEAR®

About Entrepreneur of the Year

Ernst & Young Entrepreneur of the Year® is the world's most prestigious business award for entrepreneurs. Recognised globally, the award provides a unique way of encouraging entrepreneurial activity and recognising the contribution of outstanding men and women who inspire others with their vision, leadership and achievement. As the first and only truly global award of its kind, Ernst & Young Entrepreneur of the Year® celebrates those who are building and leading successful, growing and dynamic businesses, recognising them through regional, national and global awards programmes in over 115 cities and more than 40 countries.

The Irish Ernst & Young Entrepreneur of the Year® is now in its tenth year and is run in association with the *Irish Times*, RTE, Ulster Bank, Enterprise Ireland, InterTradeIreland, Invest Northern Ireland and Digicel. The Ernst & Young Entrepreneur of the Year Case Series is compiled and edited on our behalf by the Centre for Entrepreneurship Research (CER) at Dundalk Institute of Technology. We are grateful to the CER for working with us to produce this case collection.

Enda Kelly
Partner in Charge
Entrepreneur of the Year Awards Programme

⟲ InterTradeIreland

Entrepreneurship is the spark that can set our economy alight. We need successful indigenous start-ups that can establish themselves and expand their business internationally. In Northern Ireland the private sector needs to be nurtured, and in the Republic of Ireland the challenge is to expand the domestic sector. Both require entrepreneur-led growth.

The Entrepreneur of the Year finalists provide us with valuable role models whose experience we can all learn from. These are entrepreneurs from our own towns, cities and neighbourhoods; their success should encourage us all. We hope that these case studies will help convince people who have an idea to give it a shot. The potential rewards are great.

InterTradeIreland is here to help entrepreneurs at every stage. We have designed a suite of programmes to support companies in a challenging global marketplace. InterTradeIreland can assist your business in Ireland and Northern Ireland by:

- providing support to market goods and services in another jurisdiction;
- funding cutting-edge research and development to improve global competitiveness;
- accelerating the transfer of technology into practical business applications;
- offering advice on how to raise seed and venture capital by creating a convincing business plan;
- supporting the development of business networks to enable the sharing of knowledge and expertise to achieve competitive advantage faster and cheaper.

We also make specific proposals to both governments to improve the business environment in which all firms operate.

InterTradeIreland has been involved in sponsoring the Ernst & Young Entrepreneur of the Year CEO Retreat for the past four years with the aim of developing a network of entrepreneurs across the island. This year nine of the twenty-four finalists travelled from the North, a strong indication that our all-island vision is working.

Everything we do is focused on adding value to business and we are proud of our success to date. More than 350 companies are involved in InterTradeIreland programmes each year. Since 2003 these companies have reported £100/€150 million of trade and business development value. Why not contact us and we can arrange a time to discuss how we could be of value to you.

Liam Nellis
Chief Executive
InterTradeIreland

DUNDALK INSTITUTE *of* **TECHNOLOGY**

Institiúid Teicneolaíochta Dhún Dealgan

Established in 1970, Dundalk Institute of Technology (DKIT) has become a leading provider of higher education in the north-east of Ireland. Its School of Business has established a reputation for excellence, and its graduates are acknowledged to have made a major contribution to the development of the Irish economy. From an early stage in the Business School's development, entrepreneurship and innovation have formed significant elements in its undergraduate and postgraduate programmes of learning.

In 2001, the Institute's commitment to entrepreneurship was underpinned by the establishment of the Centre for Entrepreneurship Research (CER), under the direction of Dr Colette Henry. Since its inception the CER has established itself as a national centre for independent, high-level research of relevance to business, policy-makers and academics. The Centre's research team has published a wide range of articles in the field of Entrepreneurship and related areas that have helped shape and improve enterprise support interventions. While the CER continues to add to current knowledge about entrepreneurship generally, it is now recognised as setting the agenda for female entrepreneurship research on the island of Ireland. Findings from the CER's work are disseminated, through publications and research forums, to the wider academic, research and business communities. In addition, the Centre provides research opportunities for young researchers and works towards creating an enterprise culture by informing the design of the Institute's educational programmes. In 2002, as a result of the CER's work, DKIT was cited by the European Commission as a good practice example of entrepreneurship education for its teaching of enterprise across a range of disciplines.[1] Subsequent to this, the Institute was invited to a special EU conference in Oslo[2] to discuss its entrepreneurship teaching methods.

The Ernst & Young Entrepreneur of the Year Case Series is a truly innovative educational initiative and we are proud to be associated with it. We believe that the case studies in this book will inspire entrepreneurial endeavour among students across a range of disciplines throughout the island of Ireland.

Denis Cummins

Denis Cummins
Director
Dundalk Institute of Technology

NOTES

1 European Commission (2002) 'Final Report of the Expert Group "Best Procedure" Project on Education and Training for Entrepreneurship', November, p. 51. (http://ec.europa.eu/enterprise/entrepreneurship/support_measures/training_education/education_final.pdf) [accessed 6 August 2007].

2 'Entrepreneurship Education in Europe – fostering entrepreneurial mindsets through education and learning', Oslo, 26–27 October 2006.

Acknowledgements

The *Ernst & Young Entrepreneur of the Year Case Series*© highlights the entrepreneurial pathways and strategies of successful Irish entrepreneurs. By platforming positive role models, the cases aim to foster entrepreneurial endeavour among students. The cases are based on the Ernst & Young Entrepreneur of the Year Award finalists and are edited by Dr Colette Henry at the Centre for Entrepreneurship Research, Dundalk Institute of Technology. This book is a joint initiative of Ernst & Young, InterTradeIreland and the Centre for Entrepreneurship Research (DKIT).

The editor is extremely grateful to the individual entrepreneurs and case authors who willingly gave up their time so that real entrepreneurial endeavours could be converted into a valuable learning resource. Without their cooperation and expertise this book would simply not have been possible.

Thanks are also due to Enda Kelly and Ellen Moran at Ernst & Young for providing access to such fantastic entrepreneurial stories through the Ernst & Young Entrepreneur of the Year® Award. This innovative programme has enabled the entrepreneurial pathways of successful Irish entrepreneurs to be captured and platformed for the benefit of students of entrepreneurship throughout the country.

The project team are extremely grateful to InterTradeIreland for generously providing the funding for the publishing of this book. InterTradeIreland is responsible for the promotion of trade and business on an all-island and cross-border basis.

Finally, the typesetting and administrative support provided by Blackhall Publishing is also gratefully acknowledged.

Table of Contents

List of Contributors

Naomi Birdthistle, PhD	University of Limerick, Limerick, Ireland.
Conor Carroll	University of Limerick, Limerick, Ireland.
Pauline Connolly, PhD	Institute of Public Administration, Dublin, Ireland.
Thomas M. Cooney, PhD	Dublin Institute of Technology, Dublin, Ireland.
James A. Cunningham, PhD	National University of Ireland, Galway, Ireland.
Colette Henry, PhD	Centre for Entrepreneurship Research, Dundalk Institute of Technology, Dundalk, Ireland.
Geraldine McGing	Griffith College Dublin, Dublin, Ireland.
Breda O'Dwyer	Institute of Technology Tralee, Ireland.
Colm O'Gorman, PhD	University College Dublin, Dublin, Ireland.
Sharon Porter	Northern Ireland Centre for Entrepreneurship, University of Ulster, Jordanstown, Northern Ireland.
Ann Sears	Institute of Technology Tralee, Ireland.
Lorna Treanor	Centre for Entrepreneurship Research, Dundalk Institute of Technology, Dundalk, Ireland.
Garvan Whelan	Institute of Technology Tallaght, Co. Dublin, Ireland.

Introduction

COLETTE HENRY[1]

The overwhelming importance of entrepreneurship to the economy is now recognised by academics, economists, policy-makers and practitioners throughout the world. No longer is there a need to debate the critical role of entrepreneurship education and training in helping to create the next generation of budding entrepreneurs. Rather, the emphasis is now on embedding an enterprise culture at an early stage in students' development so that they graduate, not just with an academic qualification, but also with creative and problem-solving skills, which combine to produce the 'can-do' attitude found in successful entrepreneurs. In this regard, learning from real-life entrepreneurs is possibly the best type of educational experience that we can offer our students.

The case studies in this book are based on past finalists of the Ernst & Young Entrepreneur of the Year® Award. They highlight the entrepreneurial pathways and strategies of successful entrepreneurs on the island of Ireland, and demonstrate the sorts of challenges that entrepreneurs face in their efforts to create new ventures or take over existing ones. Building on the success of the Ernst & Young Learning DVD, this book contains a total of nine cases, which collectively provide students and teachers of entrepreneurship with an important resource for exploring the entrepreneurial process.

The editor has endeavoured to bring together cases from a range of industry sectors, which adopt different approaches to describing business scenarios and highlight a variety of entrepreneurial themes suitable for individual study, in-class discussion or lively debate. In conjunction with the related set of teaching notes,[2] each case encourages the student to reflect on the entrepreneur's strategic approach, assess the challenges he/she faces, evaluate the potential opportunities and recommend an appropriate way forward.

Of course, in keeping with the dynamics of true entrepreneurial practice, many of the companies profiled in this book have developed and grown in the short space of time since the case authors completed their work. In some instances, the companies have developed significantly: the sale of Stockbyte, which attracted considerable media attention, being a particular example. In other instances, the changes that have taken place have been part of a carefully planned growth and development strategy identified by the entrepreneur from the outset and platformed by the case author. Plotting the recent changes to the case companies in this book will add a further valuable dimension to the student's educational learning experience.

The first case in this collection relates the establishment and growth of the Tuam-based company JFC Manufacturing. Operating in the plastics industry, the company produces a variety of products for use across a wide range of industry sectors. Its product portfolio includes drink bowls and feeding troughs for the agricultural industry, specialist containers and distribution bins for the materials handling and storage industry, grease traps and radon sumps for the construction industry, and road cones and definition posts for use in transportation. The company's CEO and founding entrepreneur – John Concannon – has managed to grow JFC's turnover beyond €30 million despite significant competitive pressures within the plastics industry internationally.

Daft.ie illustrates how a real-life problem led to the identification of a gap in the marketplace and fuelled the creation of an innovative new venture. Eamonn and Brian Fallon first developed the idea for their property website when one of their family was having difficulty finding rented accommodation in Dublin. The daft.ie website is now widely recognised as one of the premier players in the Irish accommodation market. The business has also expanded internationally to offer an extensive property portfolio across a range of countries including Austria, Croatia, Hungary, Slovakia and the United Kingdom, to name but a few.

Texthelp Systems in Northern Ireland is the focus of the third case. Here, the case author relates the story of the Antrim-based firm started in 1996 by the young Martin McKay. A major player in the assistive technologies market, Texthelp produces innovative software which, simply put, allows books to 'read themselves'. The company's product range helps people with learning and reading difficulties and is the UK market leader in its field, ranking an impressive number two in the USA. The company's founding entrepreneur has ambitious growth targets for Texthelp, which is now entering its most challenging phase of development.

Introduction

Dundalk-based Ovelle Pharmaceuticals represents the only female entrepreneurial story in this collection. Founded in 1934 as a privately owned family business, Ovelle was viewed as a small owner-managed business, manufacturing old-fashioned, unbranded traditional creams, such as calamine lotion, Silcock's Base and emulsifying ointments. Such products were typically sold over the counter by pharmacists all over the country and were highly regarded by GPs. When Joanna Gardiner took over as Managing Director in 2002, she spearheaded a dynamic restructuring process that gave the company's key brand – Elave – a new level of national brand recognition, and saw an unprecedented increase in sales. Since this case study was completed Ovelle has significantly expanded its online sales. It has also adopted an innovative marketing campaign through its controversial 'nothing-to-hide' advertisements, which have resulted in even further growth and development, both nationally and internationally.

Randox Laboratories Limited describes the entrepreneurial journey of Crumlin-based businessman Peter Fitzgerald. Established in 1982 following a short product development period, Randox produces a range of medical diagnostic products for the domestic and export markets. The case highlights the range of challenges encountered by Fitzgerald as he attempted to establish a niche for himself in what was, and still is, a highly competitive global marketplace. By investing heavily in research and development (R&D) and working to ambitious growth targets, Randox has registered over forty patents, has developed a client base in excess of 30,000 and exports its products to over 130 countries. This case highlights the classic dilemma of an entrepreneurial individual who has to make the bold decision to leave a secure job and embark on a dynamic and risky entrepreneurial journey. It was clearly the right decision for Peter Fitzgerald!

Established in 1997 by Jerry Kennelly, Stockbyte is the focus of the sixth case in this collection. Operating within the royalty-free stock photography sector, the company competes in a multi-billion dollar global marketplace. Essentially, Stockbyte provides high quality digital imagery to a range of clients using a highly developed filtering system, which makes it easy for customers to find what they need. Images can be filtered by price, people, gender, age, ethnicity, colour and orientation, among other categories. Customer groups include newspapers, magazines, advertising companies and large commercial organisations. While experience both as a photographer and working in the family publishing business in Kerry gave Kennelly the core technical skills he needed to establish Stockbyte, it was his creativity and commitment to his customers that has driven the business forward. Since this case was completed, Stockbyte, along with Kennelly's other core brand, Stockdisc, was sold to US giant Getty Images for $135 million.

Data Display was set up in 1979 by Kevin Neville in Ennistymon, Co. Clare. The company initially produced disco lights for the Irish market, but quickly developed from these humble beginnings to become a market leader in the design and manufacture of electronic information displays. Data Display serves a range of markets, including the multiplex cinema market, providing customised information display solutions to both domestic and international clients. The company has invested heavily in R&D to ensure its products remain competitive and at the cutting edge in terms of display solutions. A key dilemma highlighted in this case is that of succession planning and the continued successful management of a family business.

Griffith College Dublin, the penultimate case in this book, is the largest independent third level educational institution in the Republic of Ireland. Established in the early 1970s, Griffith grew from delivering accountancy education to small groups of students in a makeshift class-room to a world-renowned educational college with in excess of 7,000 students. The entrepreneur behind Griffith's phenomenal success is Diarmuid Hegarty, a former accountant and tax consultant. This case plat-forms the many challenges that Hegarty had to face in his attempts to keep Griffith afloat in the early years of its development and illustrates how a true entrepreneur can not only overcome significant challenges, but can also turn them into valuable opportunities for the business. Succession planning is again highlighted as a key issue in this case, along with the incredible drive, dedication and forward thinking of a real entrepreneur.

The final case in our E & Y Entrepreneur of the Year Case Series is Chain Reaction Cycles. The third of our Northern Ireland-based entrepre-neurs profiled in this collection, Christopher Watson, took over his par-ents' small family business in 1990 and turned it into a major global supplier of mountain bikes with customers in over 100 countries. Chris developed the business' mail order service into a major web-based order-ing facility, using the domain name www.chainreactioncycles.com. Rapid expansion has seen the business utilising some 12,500 square feet of space to maintain its stock. While essentially an e-based retailer of mountain bikes, bike parts and related clothing and footwear, Chain Reaction Cycles is continuously diversifying by offering associated products such as snow-boarding equipment. It is no wonder that it is now Europe's largest online bike store.

This text should become a valuable resource for both teachers and students of entrepreneurship in helping to identify the pathways and strategies of established Irish entrepreneurs, thus providing real insights into the new venture creation and management process. As Denis O'Brien, Chairman of Digicel, has already highlighted in his foreword to this book, starting small ventures is just as important as starting big ones. Learning from each other will provide us with insights to both.

Dr Colette Henry
Director
Centre for Entrepreneurship Research

NOTES

1   Dr Colette Henry is Head of Department of Business Studies and Director of the Centre for Entrepreneurship Research (CER) at Dundalk Institute of Technology.
2   The teaching notes associated with these cases are available from Ernst & Young to teachers and lecturers on request.

John Concannon
JFC[1]

James A. Cunningham[2]

INTRODUCTION

It is approaching eight o'clock on a Tuesday evening and John
Concannon, founder and CEO of JFC, is on an Aer Lingus flight bound
for Dublin from Warsaw. His thoughts turn to preparing a presentation
that he has agreed to give to budding entrepreneurs at the Radisson Hotel
in Galway the following morning. The co-pilot's announcement inter-
rupts his thoughts: "the flight will arrive on time in Dublin airport". This
is good news, as he will be on time for his connecting 10.15 p.m. Aer
Arann flight to Galway. He reaches for his A4 pad and his bag, and
begins to jot down some notes for tomorrow morning's presentation. In
doing so he reflects on his experiences – the highs as well as the difficult
times. He casts his mind back to when the company was first founded in
1987, when the industrial outlook in Tuam was bleak. In January of that
year the town experienced the closure of the local sugar factory, which
had provided employment for the whole community. As a result, the
unemployment rate in the Tuam area hit 28.8 per cent. There is no doubt
that he has come a long way since then. As his flight nears the end of its
journey, John looks through the airplane window at the green fields
below and thinks about what he will say in his presentation. A turnover
in excess of €30 million, a workforce of 200 and operations in the UK,
Poland and the Netherlands are all evidence of his company's phenomenal success. But the challenge of remaining innovative in a cost-driven
and highly competitive marketplace is always at the forefront of John's
mind.

The Entrepreneurial Journey – The Early Years

John Concannon was educated in St Jarleth's in Tuam and, on leaving school, worked in the transport industry and helped out on the family farm for nearly ten years. However he wanted to educate himself further and do something different with his life. He set about undertaking night courses in marketing and psychology, and reading about business and business people who had set up their own businesses. His first real business venture was selling smoke alarms door-to-door based on a bank loan of IR£1,000. He only sold one smoke alarm, but he learned a key lesson – the need for effective sales and marketing techniques. Such techniques have become key ingredients in the growth of JFC. He then went on a professional selling course while working on the family farm, which provided the inspiration for his first product idea – a plastic-based feeding system for cattle – which essentially combined three feeding buckets. Concannon describes the moment as:

> I was feeding calves one day and though the job could get done more quickly if I fixed three buckets together.... Other farmers saw the idea and wanted something similar, so I refined the design and got a plastics manufacturer to make the bucket.[3]

He twice attempted to raise funding from IDA Ireland at the time; he was refused but received a grant of IR£1,800 from the Country Enterprise Board, which allowed him to buy some tools to finish off the plastic products that Rom Plastics had manufactured for him. Selling his feeding system was tough in the Galway region, so he decided to base himself in Listowel, Co. Kerry, where he set himself a target of twenty units per day selling to farmers. This proved successful, but he had yet to break into the co-op market, which was proving difficult in terms of getting a supplier code. Driving back from Kerry he stopped at the Mitchelstown Co-op in Garryspillane, Co. Limerick, where he gave a sales presentation. He succeeded in overcoming the co-op bureaucracy by becoming a supplier and getting a universal supplier code. In 1986, before formally setting up JFC, he won the Premier Award for Innovation at the RDS Spring Show, and an appearance on the *Late Late Show* helped increase the profile of the product.

JFC's first premises were in the Dunmore Road Industrial Estate in Tuam, where Concannon installed the first rotational moulding machine. The British Plastics Association describes rotational moulding as a process used to produce hollow plastic products and consists of four phases of production: charging mould, heating and fusion, cooling, and unloading and de-moulding (see Exhibit 1). This process provides the advantages of economically produced large products, minimum design constraints, stress-free products and low moulding costs.

As activity increased Concannon purchased machinery from Grolly Dolls in Donegal for IR£4,000, which was one-tenth of their original value. Two years later the business moved to Weir Road, JFC's current location, as it had bought more machines in Scotland and needed additional space to store them. JFC began to recruit some of the engineers who had worked in the sugar factory to assist with the configuration of the machines and with new product development. Concannon's sales and marketing skills came to the fore as JFC attended various agricultural shows and other trade events, which offered opportunities not only to sell products, but also to keep up with trends and happenings in the industry. These shows also allowed John to scout for talent in his quest for international expansion in the UK, mainland Europe and Poland.

PRODUCT DEVELOPMENT AND INNOVATIONS

In 2005 the company turnover reached €30 million, based on a doubling of the company size in the previous years and sales of a range of products to various markets, including transport, equestrian, hospitality, materials handling, medical, agriculture, environment, road building and the construction industry (see Exhibits 2 and 3). This proliferation of product ranges was possible because the company has invested heavily in research and development (R&D), spending over €1 million in dedicated facilities, with support from Enterprise Ireland and ten dedicated R&D staff. Concannon acknowledges this:

> R&D has delivered products and processes that have given us the advantage over the competition…. For a small company to have 10 people in R&D is expensive but JFC are getting the return on their investment.[4]

Such diversification and proliferation in new product development was in reaction to the identified decline in the agriculture market, as well as the seasonality of the products JFC sold into this market.

JFC has some notable world-class product innovations. For example, the CorriPipe™ was developed as a result of Concannon's visit to Kavanagh's Foundry in Birr, Co. Offaly, where they use recycled metal to manufacture their products. On the way back to Galway, Concannon passed trucks delivering concrete piping to Bord na Móna. From this visit, JFC developed a twin wall, high-density polyethylene pipe that is made completely from waste plastics, such as drink and shampoo bottles, and other suitable plastics. The advantages over existing concrete products is that there are reduced planning and labour costs associated with its laying, as it comes in six metre lengths, thereby reducing the joins, and can be easily cut to size. The CorriPipe™ is used for civil engineering, construction, agriculture and other sub-soil applications. This product has been used as part of the drainage system for sports fields and golf courses. As Concannon explains:

> ...The company's recycled corrugated drainage pipe – CorriPipe™ – has found favour with local authorities around Ireland. To date, the pipes have been used in major bypass construction projects in Drogheda, Sligo and Letterkenny. We are also negotiating for the supply of drainage pipes for the Naas bypass. It is great to be supplying pipes for all these major road construction initiatives, and we are also very proud that Galway County Council are using our CorriPipes™, which are made in the Tuam plant, for all major road building schemes.[5]

With the implementation of EU directives on water management legislation, and an increase in flooding in Europe due to climate change, JFC developed the HydroCell™, which is used in the building of an underground stormwater storage tank, designed, supplied and installed on-site by JFC. Concannon explains:

> HydroCell is used where there are problems with flash flooding. This product is a cost-effective way of alleviating flash flooding and in the storage of water underground.[6]

Camtech Environmental Ltd, based in Shropshire in the UK, manufactures Casflo Packaged Sewage Treatment Systems, Proplex Pumping Systems, Kiosks and Housing, 'Fastrippa' Grease Interceptors and Standard Grease Traps, Process Vessels and Special Fabrications. The Casflo Sewage Treatment System is designed for applications where the installation of septic tanks is either impractical or unacceptable and a connection to the main sewer system is impossible. JFC has developed a number of patented features that ensure the simplicity of the operation while meeting the stringent guidelines of environmental protection agencies, and its products can be installed by a building contractor. More recent products have been developed in terms of plastic vehicle protective inserts, which protects the inside of 4X4 and other commercial vehicles. These products are available, for example, in Nissan Patrol/Terranos, Toyota Land Cruisers, Isuzu Troopers and Mitsubishi Pajeros and pick-up trucks.

With its approved ISO 9001-2000 standard, and its experience in plastic mould making, JFC has developed the capability to develop custom mouldings for customers from idea through to design and on to production. Such experience has meant that JFC has been able to recently develop aquaculture products for fish farms, and now has the world market for the product based on its patented design. This development resulted from undertaking unsolicited, customised moulding work for client companies in Bulgaria. In addition to undertaking custom moulding, JFC also undertakes contract component production as it makes, for example, plastic covers and parts for McHale, Tanco, O'Donovan Engineering and Larkin Engineering. As Conconnon explains:

> Because we design and develop everything in-house we are able to make a small number of items that can be rigorously tested before full-scale production. We make all the machine tools and moulds to minimize costs, so if something is wrong with the design, the fault is traced and rectified.[7]

INTERNATIONAL EXPANSION

The international expansion of JFC has been relatively small in scale and has been built through market knowledge of people and competing products.

Expansions in both Holland and Poland have come through personal contacts developed through attendance at international trade fairs, with initial operations being run out of apartments. The attendance at international trade fairs serves the dual purpose of selling JFC products and keeping a focus on market developments and changes. JFC's footprint outside of Ireland includes sales and distribution offices in Shropshire (UK), Surhuisterveen (Holland) and Dabrowka (Poland) (see Exhibit 4).

For the first eleven years of its operation, JFC was focused on agri-products, but the foot-and-mouth crisis and BSE scares hit the company severely:

> Until 1998, we relied solely on agricultural products and we were exporting to the UK and mainland Europe. It was around this time that the agricultural sector was hit by a number of significant setbacks and the market went into decline. It taught us not to fully rely on one market.

JFC now exports to over thirty countries, including America, Japan, Korea and Australia, and continues to attend national and international trade shows (see Exhibit 5), with these exports accounting for over 60 per cent of the company's total sales.

JFC's first international acquisition was PD Roto Mouldings, an established UK company that had experienced some decline in fortunes. The attractiveness of this company was its customer base that it had build up over decades, which JFC successfully exploited to develop a presence in the UK market. In 2004, JFC won the *Sunday Business Post* Deal of the Year for its €5 million acquisition of Delleve Plastics and the Reprise Plastic Recycling firms in St Helens in the UK. Delleve Plastics recycles polyethylene and PET (polyethylene terephthalate). A further investment of €3 million in raising its capacity ensures that it will become one of the largest recyclers in the UK by 2007. It will also have the capacity to reprocess 44 million pounds of plastic per year – a significant increase from its base of 17.6 million pounds in 2004. This additional investment was part funded by a grant of STG£1.8 million from the British Waste Resource Action Plan (WRAP), which contributed to the development of automated sorting equipment which sorts bottles by colour and density. The recycled plastic is used by Delleve in the production of corrugated pipes and, in 2004, a further investment of €1.2 million led to the installation of an extrusion line, which allows Delleve to manufacture twin-wall corrugated pipes up to 23.6 inches in diameter. According to Concannon:

> The potential for expansion [in bottle recycling] is huge and the markets for corrugated pipes across Europe are also growing at an enormous rate, as they are fast replacing concrete pipes in the construction and drainage projects. We are pleased with our progress to date. We want to expand our business. If we had not turned things around, the Delleve business wouldn't work well here today.[8]

However, there is still further growth potential in this market, as only 62 per cent of UK local authorities collect plastic bottles, and less than 10 per cent of these bottles are then recycled.

In 2005, JFC acquired Knotwood Composites in St Helens in the UK for €1.5 million, which added to JFC's product portfolio of outdoor furniture, fencing and decking. This product division was re-branded as JFC Delta Decking and Fencing, as Concannon explained:

> We see tremendous potential, especially on the international markets, for this latest range of items added to our ever-growing catalogue. The Delta Decking and Fencing products are long-lasting and maintenance-free. They are attractive and economical for the customers, while their manufacture from a mixture of recycled plastic and waste wood makes them environmentally friendly too.[9]

In 2004, in tandem with these acquisitions, JFC opened a manufacturing plant in Poland about twenty kilometres from Warsaw, which represented a €4 million investment. The plant was opened by the Minister of State for European Affairs Mr Noel Tracey and the Polish Ambassador. As Concannon explains:

> We had to create a new product range which would be suitable for the Polish market and culture. We also had a language and distance barrier to overcome, but so far the results have been fantastic and our Polish plant is operating well ahead of targets.

By 2006, the Polish plant employed ten people and had two moulding machines in operation. The cost of the Polish operation is currently running at one-fifth of its Irish counterpart.

THE PLASTICS INDUSTRY

While the Old Testament has references to natural materials such as filler, adhesives and coatings that were the precursors of the modern plastic materials industry, the exact year in which the plastics industry began is still debated among historians. Interestingly, the history of the rubber industry has a bearing on plastics, with hard rubber being discovered in 1851, which involved a distinct chemical modification of a natural material. However, it was not until 1927 that cellulose acetate, a thermoplastic, was introduced as a moulding compound and the 1930s saw the initial commercial application of thermoplastics: polyvinyl chloride, low-density polyethylene, polystyrene and polymethyl methacryle. World War II accelerated the demand for plastics due to the shortages of natural materials. Plastics are now used in a wide variety of industry sectors including, for example, consumer goods, furniture, construction and electronics, where there are about fifty different groups of plastics, with hundreds of different varieties. The American Society of Plastics developed standard marking codes to assist consumers identify and sort the main types of plastics (see Exhibit 6), with plastic consumption in Europe growing by 4 per cent per year and making up approximately 7 per cent of the average household dustbin.

In 2004 the plastics industry in the US was fourth among the top manufacturing industry groups, and accounted for 3.4 million jobs and $438 billion in shipments. The world's annual consumption of plastic materials increased from three million tonnes in the 1950s to over 100 million this decade, with Asia producing 44 million tonnes. Take for example the $800 billion packaging industry: plastics form an important material type in the flexible packaging market (bubble wrap, stand-up pouches, etc.), with over 70 per cent market share in European and North American markets. In the UK approximately six million tonnes of plastic products are used in different sectors of the economy, with packaging representing the largest single consumer of plastics (see Exhibit 7). The increase in energy costs has placed UK plastic manufacturers under increased competitive pressure, with the British Plastics Federation reporting in a survey that 44 per cent of its members were not in a position to pass on these increased energy costs to their customers in their selling prices, as Davis outlines:

> Last October, member firms incurred average increases of 58 per cent for gas, and 56 per cent for electricity. Many firms were faced with a staggering 100 per cent rise. Companies will go to the wall if they cannot secure any relief from this.[10]

The Irish plastics industry employs 9,000 people providing products for a range of different industry sectors such as medical devices, automotive parts, consumer electronics, frozen food packaging and telecommunications equipment. An IBEC survey[11] of the industry reported that 60 per cent of respondents expressed confidence about the future of the industry up to 2008.

Overall, the worldwide plastics industry is facing an uncertain future, with increasing oil prices and weak consumer demand. The traditionally strong market for plastic resins (polypropylene (PP) and polyethylene terephalate (PET)) reported poor sales in 2005, attributable to their usages in the food and beverage industry.

The construction and agricultural machinery markets are among the key sectors in which JFC competes. Market growth in Europe has been sluggish, with no growth in this sector until 2004. A market growth rate of 4.6 per cent in 2004 valued the industry at $28.8 billion, with agricultural machinery accounting for 53 per cent of the market value.[12] By the year 2009, industry analysts expect the market to have grown to $30 billion. The UK market for construction and agricultural machinery has faired better in recent years, with a compounded annual growth rate of 2.2 per cent from 2000 to 2004, with agricultural machinery accounting for 71 per cent of the market share. Industry forecasts indicate that this sector will only grow by 1.3 per cent by 2009, valuing it at $5 billion. The global environmental and facilities services market also grew by 4.3 per cent, with solid waste management activities recording a market share of 51.8 per cent and an estimated value of $102 billion. In global terms, the US accounts for 40 per cent, with Europe accounting for 31 per cent of market value. The sector is forecast to grow by 4.5 per cent year-on-year up to 2009, with its value doubling to $247.3 billion.

THE FUTURE

The plane begins its decent to Dublin airport. The rich orange glow of the evening sunset lights up the plane's cabin. Reflecting on the last eighteen months and on the many miles travelled, Concannon is pleased with JFC's export drive of equestrian products to East Asia, and with his successes in attempting to gain market share for its thermal plastic water troughs in Norway, Finland and Sweden. In 2001 JFC was involved in the DHL Export Awards and in 2005 the company was awarded the Best Environment Initiative from the British Plastics Association. Also in 2005, John Concannon was selected as one of the finalists in the Ernst & Young Entrepreneur of the Year Award.

New product development continues apace with pipefittings and accessories for CorriPipe™ (certified by the British Board of Agrimont), mussel floats and plastic products for the Salvation Army and water treatment equipment. Anticipating the type of questions that he will be asked after his presentation to the group of budding entrepreneurs, Concannon reflects on the major issues facing the company. The ongoing rapid expansion will mean that JFC faces the challenge of maintaining a small entrepreneurial company culture and balancing this with developing an organisational infrastructure and human capital that will support growth. As with previous presentations about JFC, Concannon is again keen for this event to highlight the role of his staff at JFC and their role in growing the business:

> It's a great credit to the staff and the whole team working at JFC that, through their efforts, our group, with its headquarters in the west of Ireland, continues to expand its activities internationally.... Staff are encouraged to feel that they are vital cogs in an organisation which is constantly expanding.

Successful international expansion in the UK and Poland has tested the management team. The JFC culture, as well as changes in the legislative environment, has provided some new market opportunities. The rise in fuel prices and the bulky nature of some of the products provide ongoing challenges for JFC. In meeting these challenges, Concannon knows that he needs to focus on nurturing and developing managerial talent in order to bring JFC through the next phases of international expansion. Like any other business in this situation, the issue of succession comes to mind. The future offers opportunities to diversify into new product areas and for further acquisitions. As the aircraft is about to touch the ground, Concannon is thinking of the words that he will use for tomorrow's presentation which can best summarise the future challenges for JFC. As the air hostess begins to welcome passengers to Dublin and the plane taxis to its gate, Concannon jots down, "the future challenge for JFC is *continuously hammering home the difference*."

NOTES

1 This case was prepared by Dr James A. Cunningham as the basis for class discussion rather than to illustrate either effective or ineffective handling of a business situation.
2 James Cunningham lectures in the J.E. Cairnes Graduate School of Business and Public Policy, National University of Ireland, Galway (james.cunningham@nuigalway.ie). The author is extremely grateful to John Concannon for his time and his co-operation in helping to prepare this case.
3 Concannon, J. (2002) 'Barrows on tow, bins on the move', *Farmers' Guardian*, 20 September, p. 7.
4 Ernst & Young (2005) 'Ernst & Young 2005 Entrepreneur of the Year Awards', *JFC Manufacturing*, available at <http://www.jfc.ie/index.asp?active_page_id=5> [accessed 30 August 2006].
5 Concannon, J. (2004) 'JFC's €5M Plant Deals', *Sunday Business Post*, 26 December.
6 Concannon, 2004.
7 Concannon, 2002.
8 Concannon, 2004.
9 Ernst & Young, 2005.
10 Davis, P. (2006) 'Plastics Industry's Plea on Energy Bill', *News Digest*, 9 February.
11 IBEC (2004) 'Plastics Sector Potential Outlined in Survey', Press Release 6 December 2004, *IBEC*, available at <http://www.ibec.ie/ibec/press/presspublicationsdoclib3.nsf/wvPCICCC/4317CD96744E3B8C80256F5F00601BCF?OpenDocument> [accessed 30 August 2006].
12 Datamonitor (2005) *Construction & Farm Machinery in Europe: Industry Profile*, London, p. 10.

Exhibit 1
The Rotational Moulding Process

Charging Mould
A pre-determined amount of polymer powder is placed in the mould. With the powder loaded, the mould is closed, locked and loaded into the oven. The powder can be pre-compounded to the desired colour.

Heating and Fusion
Once inside the oven, the mould is rotated around two axes, tumbling the powder – the process is not a centrifugal one. The speed of rotation is relatively slow, less than 20 rev/min. The ovens are heated by convection, conduction and, in some cases, radiation. As the mould becomes hotter the powder begins to melt and stick to the inner walls of the mould. As the powder melts, it gradually builds up an even coating over the entire surface.

Cooling
When the melt has been consolidated to the desired level, the mould is cooled by air, water or a combination of both. The polymer solidifies to the desired shape.

Unloading/De-moulding
When the polymer has cooled sufficiently to retain its shape and be easily handled, the mould is opened and the product removed. At this point powder can once again be placed in the mould and the cycle repeated.

Exhibit 2
JFC Product Categories and Listings

Product Category	Sample List of Products
Agri-Products	Drink Bowls, Water Troughs, Dairy Hygiene, Feed Troughs, Calf Hutches, Feed Equipment, Footbaths, Equine Equipments, ATV Tipping Trailers, Wheel Barrows, Accessories
Materials Handling and Storage	IBCs, Durabins, Transitanks, Haztanks, Distribution Trolley Range, Spring Lift Trolley, Distribution Bins, General Containers, Drums and Containers, Polytanks
Laundry	Standard Linen Trolleys, Customised Linen Trolleys
Recycling/Environment	Bottle Banks, Waste Oil Storage, Alu Foil Bank, Drink Can Banks, Battery Banks
Construction	Surface and Stormwater Drainage Solutions, Gullies, BioMedia, Grease Trap, Radon Sumps
Oil Storage	Oil Tanks 1,100 litres and 1,500 litres, Slim Line tanks, Bunded Tanks
Transport	Road Bollards, Junction Definition Posts, Road Cones

Source: <http://www.jfc.ie>

Exhibit 3
Examples of JFC's Product Range

Exhibit 4
The JFC Group

Activity/Location	Website
JFC Manufacturing (Europe) UK Sales and Distribution Office – PD Roto Mouldings (Oswestry, Shropshire, UK)	www.jfcuk.com
JFC Delleve Plastic Recyclers, Reprocessors and Manufacturers (Warwickshire, UK)	www.delleve.co.uk
JFC Poloska SP Polish Sales and Manufacturing Office	www.jfcpolska.com
Dutch Sales and Distribution Office	www.jfceurope.com
Plastic Recycling Plant (St Helens, Merseyside, UK)	www.delleve.co.uk
Camtech Environmental Ltd (Telford, Shropshire, UK)	www.camtechenvironmental.com

Exhibit 5
International and National Trade Fair Attendance 2006

March
8 March: Irish Waste Water and Environment Show, Dublin, Ireland
May
10–11 May: Balmoral Show, Kings Hall, Belfast, Northern Ireland
June
14–16 June: Attended by JFC UK Office – CIWM Recycling Exhibition, Torquay, Devon, UK
July
18–21 July: Attended by JFC UK Office – Royal Welsh Agricultural Show, Builth Wells, Pows, Wales
August
13 August: Tullamore Show, Charleville Estate, Tullamore, Co. Offaly, Ireland
September
21–22 September: Attended by JFC UK Office – National Agricultural Centre, Stonleigh, Warwickshire, UK
27–30 September: National Ploughing Championships, Tullow, Co. Carlow, Ireland
22–25: Attended by JFC Holland Office – Agro Expo, Ismir, Turkey
October
14 October: National Dairy Show, The Green Glens Show Complex, Millstreet, Co. Cork, Ireland
19–20 October: Attended by JFC UK Office – Fencing and Landscaping News Exhibition, the Newark Showground, Newark-on-Trent, UK
27–29 October: Attended by JFC Holland Office – Kone Agria, Jyvaskyla, Finland
November
9–11 November: Plan Expo (Stand A5), RDS Simmonscourt, Dublin, Ireland
December
13 December: Royal Ulster Winter Fair, Kings Hall, Belfast, Northern Ireland

Source: <http://www.jfc.ie>

Exhibit 6
Plastic Types by Common Usage

ASP Symbol	Name	Usage
PET	Polyethylene terephthalate	Fizzy drink bottles and oven ready meal trays
HDPE	High-density polyethylene	Bottles for milk and washing-up liquids
PVC	Polyvinyl chloride	Food trays, cling film, bottles of squash, mineral water and shampoo
LDPE	Low density polyethylene	Carrier bags and bin liners
PP	Polypropylene	Margarine tubs and microwaveable meal trays
PS	Polystyrene	Yoghurt pots, foam meat or fish trays, hamburger boxes, egg cartons, vending cups, plastic cutlery, protective packaging for electronic goods and toys

Exhibit 7
UK Plastics Consumption by Sector (2005)

Sector	Consumption as a Percentage
Packaging	35%
Building and Construction	23%
Electrical and Electronics	8%
Furniture/Houseware	8%
Transport	8%
Agriculture	7%
Toys/Sport	3%
Mechanical Engineering	2%
Medical	2%
Footwear	1%
Others	3%

Source: British Plastics Association

Eamonn and Brian Fallon Daft.ie[1]

Thomas M. Cooney[2]

Introduction

Eamonn and Brian Fallon sat in their office at the Digital Hub near the Guinness Brewery in Dublin and reflected upon their success. About them on the walls was an array of awards that they had collected over the past two years. Indeed, they had received a telephone call earlier that day informing them that the radio programme 'Down To Business' on NewsTalk 106 had selected them as a leading example of best business practice and wanted to interview them. It was yet further recognition that the decisions that they had taken in the past were paying rich dividends. The company's website <http://www.daft.ie> was now receiving over 650,000 unique visitors a month and it was generally regarded as being Ireland's biggest property website.

Different types of competitors had noted the Fallons' success and were looking to eat into their market. Eamonn and Brian started to brainstorm as to what their growth options might be: (1) go international, (2) develop the area of overseas property, (3) upsell opportunities for existing customers, (4) develop the commercial property sector, (5) have other classifieds such as jobs and motors, (6) develop different language versions for foreign nationals coming to work in Ireland, (7) develop the mortgage centre activities and (8) place a greater focus on the advertisers rather than the users. While each of these options had merits, they also had negative aspects. The Fallons had created their success by being completely focused on their product and service offering, spending only retained funding to finance growth, and using word-of-mouth as their solitary promotional tool. While they did not want to alter these principles, they recognised that growing the

25

business would require significant changes. It felt like their success was causing them more difficulties than solutions, and that the challenges they faced were getting bigger and bigger.

BACKGROUND TO THE COMPANY

The idea for Daft.ie initially arose from a discussion around the Fallon family dinner table. One of the members of the family was leaving home and was looking for rented accommodation in Dublin. It was 1997 and the principal way of finding rented property at that time was through the classified advertisements in the newspapers. However, there were a number of limitations with this system, the greatest of which was that the advertisement gave very limited information regarding the property. To secure suitable accommodation required many telephone calls and visits, sometimes taking weeks to find a suitable property. But the system was also inefficient for landlords as they had to take a block booking for three days and, although the property may be taken after the first day, people would continue to make contact over the following two days. It was generally an unsatisfactory way of doing business for both parties; the only alternative was to go through an agency and that was more expensive.

Around that time Indigo had launched a consumer Internet package and the Fallon brothers had purchased one as a gift for their father. However, they soon realised that he was not interested in using it so they started to explore the benefits of it themselves. Eamonn had also just started an engineering degree course at Trinity College Dublin and so wanted to know more about this new channel of information. It was the early days of the Internet and its uses were still narrow, with limited information available. They researched the Internet looking for websites that had a real-time list of properties, with photographs and extended information, and with the date on which the property was entered. Trawling through the different search engines revealed that no such website existed for Ireland and, together with the discussion around the family dinner table, they realised that they had identified a real business opportunity.

Nothing happened for some time as Eamonn pursued his studies in engineering at university and Brian was still at second-level education. However, a business ideas competition for second-level students prompted Brian to explore the possibility of using the online properties idea for his business plan, and so he started to develop a very basic website. He began by building a homepage that offered two options: house sharing and property to let. For a number of months people would email their requests to brian@indigo.ie and he would copy and paste them onto the website, where they remained until such time as the property was taken. It was a free listing service and the website was promoted by Eamonn through posters, primarily located in the third level colleges about the city. The only income stream was through business advertising, but that remained small for a considerable time. Brian reached the final of the competition but people's lack of understanding at that time of how the Internet worked did not help his chances of success. However, more heartening was the discovery that a very large accountancy firm in Dublin was telling its new recruits to check out the website when looking for property, as this endorsement took its target market away from the student market for the first time.

The website used a variety of domain names during the early days, including <http://www.indigo.ie/brian> and <http://www.property.tp>. In 1999 they finally took the name Daft.ie when they realised that the opportunity was more substantial than they had ever imagined and a definite brand name needed to be established. A highly reputable estate agent had been frantically calling Brian at his secondary school wanting him to upload properties urgently as customer demand was requiring a fast turnaround in properties to let. This demand for the website also coincided with Eamonn finishing his studies at university and so he began to spend more time working on the business. He was also working for a web consultancy business at that time which allowed him the opportunity to build up his knowledge and database of people within the Internet industry. The website was totally revamped at the end of 1999 to give it a more professional look and this remained until 2004.

Until late 1999 the website was a small niche player getting approximately 5,000 hits per month. However, with the revamping of the website, the change in name to Daft.ie and the decision to go nationwide with its services, the company suddenly began to grow quite quickly. It was still a free-listing website with the only revenue stream coming from banner advertising. The growth of the business, however, was supported by the dot.com boom in the early years of the new millennium, but despite the tales of fabulous wealth being generated by Internet entrepreneurs the Fallon brothers decided to grow the business organically. They felt that the Internet industry needed to settle down and mature before they would consider making any large investments in the firm.

It was September 2003 before Eamonn joined the business in a full-time capacity, with Brian following in the summer of 2004. The company initially employed one part-time person in December 2003, but since then has expanded to employing ten full-time employees. As part of the development of the business the company needed to improve its customer service capability and so dedicated one employee to give a customised response to every email that it received, as well as delivering other highly-tailored emails to all of its different types of users. It also added features such as a time-delay to give the impression that automatically generated responses had been highly considered and that the company had a large support team. As part of its customer service strategy it was not prepared to pay large sums of money for above-the-line advertising for its website, and so it focused on word-of-mouth promotion. It sought to "build a community" of people who would tell their friends about the service in much the same manner as eBay. It now has 350,000 registered users who, the Fallons believe, act as advocates for their services. But the expansion of the business had not gone unnoticed in the wider community either, for in 2004 the Fallon brothers were rewarded for their efforts by being nominated as finalists for the very prestigious Ernst & Young Entrepreneur of the Year Awards. They have since gone on to receive an array of awards, including four Golden Spider Awards in 2004 and the Small Business of the Year Award in 2005. Interestingly, these awards have also given the company significant promotion without the need to spend any money.

CURRENT ACTIVITIES

Daft.ie is now not only Ireland's largest property website, but also the busiest website. An independent audit of Internet traffic by ABC ELECTRONIC confirmed that Daft.ie received requests for over 27 million pages of information (page impressions) in May 2006, the largest ABC ELECTRONIC audited figure for any Irish website to date. These figures make Daft.ie Ireland's busiest certified website at 17 July 2006, ahead of other well-known sites, including RTE.ie (22 million, May 2006), Eircom.net (22 million, January 2006) and MyHome.ie (18 million, October 2005) (see Exhibit 1).[3]

These figures are even more impressive when you consider the population of Ireland. For example, Daft.ie delivers twice as many page impressions per head of population as the biggest online property site in the UK (see Exhibit 2). This is a good indication of how comfortable Irish people have become at using the Internet to buy, sell and rent property online. Management believes that the success of the company has been based on its ability to grow with its original audience. Whereas once Daft.ie was the first port of call for students looking for a room to rent, almost ten years on the website now helps them buy a new home, rent an office or purchase a property abroad.

The company delivers these 27 million pages of properties a month to over 1,300,000 visitors, with more than 40,000 properties to sell or let at any one time. The company also has over 1,000 estate agents and approximately 45,000 landlords/homeowners advertising regularly on the website. The company has expanded its original accommodation offerings of sales, lettings and sharing to also include short-term, commercial and overseas properties. It is this combination of broad property offerings that makes it unique within the Irish marketplace. More recently, it has also created a mortgage centre as an additional feature that allows users to apply online for a mortgage. The company also offers parking spaces for rental, reflecting the increased demand for this facility in the major cities of Ireland. Indeed, when a person rents a property from Daft.ie a list of parking spaces available nearby is automatically generated for the user.

A major change in recent times for the company is that the revenue streams for the business have been extended beyond the original banner advertising fees. While that income stream remains quite strong, the business now receives income from a wider variety of sources, including fees paid by estate agents and landlords for advertising their properties, and sponsorship from property-related companies such as mortgage and insurance businesses. Interestingly, despite the additional income streams and customer markets, the company remains faithful to its policy of not having above-the-line advertising (even when Daft.ie enters into new markets), which means that its marketing costs are kept quite low. Simultaneously, one of the most effective marketing tools developed by the company in recent times has been the Daft.ie Quarterly Property Report, which is an analysis of recent trends in the Irish rental market. The report is used by the Central Bank, mortgage institutions, financial analysts and by the general public as the most definitive barometer of movements in that particular market.

The original business concept for Daft.ie was based around accommodation letting and sharing. While Eamonn Fallon believes that the company has no direct competitors, he does accept that the company has many indirect competitors. Apart from word-of-mouth, evening newspapers such as the *Evening Herald* and *Galway Advertiser* remain the major opposition for the letting market, although there is some evidence of newspapers moving this element of their activities online also. The management of Daft.ie believe that the company retains the same advantages over newspapers as it did when it started almost ten years ago, and that these newspapers cannot compete with the breadth and depth of properties offered by Daft.ie. Other competitors for Daft.ie would include traditional letting agencies (such as Home Locators in Dublin) that also have their properties on their own websites. Again none of these agencies would have the number of properties offered by Daft.ie. These agencies, however, would also advertise their properties on Daft.ie, and so they are both customer and competitor at the same time. Brian Fallon estimates that in excess of 90 per cent of the rental properties in Ireland will be found on Daft.ie and therefore these types of traditional letting agencies cannot be legitimately classified as a competitor.

Research by the company has discovered that its users remain very loyal, and so, as they traded up the property ladder, they returned to Daft.ie for help. Because of the strength of this relationship, the house sales element of Daft.ie was launched in 2003 and it has become particularly strong amongst first-time buyers as the transition is made by users from accommodation rental to home purchase. The general public would perceive that the biggest online operator for house sales is MyHome.ie, which has a strong brand name and a good market presence. However, it does not have the range of property activities (i.e. sales, lettings, sharing, short-term, commercial and overseas properties) offered by Daft.ie. This would also be true for its other competitors in this market, such as PropertyPartners.ie and SherryFitz.ie. However, management recognises that, within the house sales market, these websites have an excellent reputation and are more likely to be many people's first destination when looking to buy a house, as Daft.ie is still generally considered to be primarily in the accommodation rental market. However, both brothers do not believe that these types of websites are direct competitors with Daft.ie.

As part of the services for those users wishing to trade-up or extend their property portfolio, Daft.ie introduced foreign properties as a natural extension of its services to its clients. By June 2006, it offered properties in all of the following countries:

- Europe:
  Austria, Belgium, Bulgaria, Croatia, Cyprus, Czech Republic, Estonia, France, Germany, Greece, Holland, Hungary, Italy, Latvia, Lithuania, Malta, Poland, Portugal, Romania, Serbia and Montenegro, Slovakia, Slovenia, Spain, Turkey, United Kingdom.
- North America/Central America/South America:
  Brazil, Canada, Caribbean Islands, Dominican Republic, Panama, Peru, United States.
- Middle East:
  United Arab Emirates.
- Asia/Oceania:
  Australia, China, India, Indonesia, New Zealand, Thailand.
- Africa:
  Cape Verde, Morocco, South Africa.

The overseas properties are supplied by foreign partners who view the Irish market as a wonderful opportunity for holiday home investment. The overseas property element of the business clearly demonstrates the key strengths of the management team within Daft.ie: a willingness to develop new target markets, relationship building with new partners, innovation in terms of product offering and a continual desire to enhance the value that it brings to its users. Interestingly, one of the customer groups for overseas properties is the landlords who have previously advertised their Irish properties through Daft.ie. They are now seeking further investment opportunities and overseas property is a natural progression for them.

Another development with regard to international linkages is the development of partnership agreements with websites that are focused on sending workers to Ireland (such as recruitment agencies in Poland and other eastern European countries). These websites offer links to Daft.ie's accommodation lettings section, thus enabling the user to find accommodation before they arrive in Ireland. This new form of advertising, which is an advert and user link at the same time, allows the company to develop a new group of customers from outside the usual target markets. As with previous users, once they have established themselves in Ireland and are seeking to purchase their own home, they will hopefully continue to use the broad product and service offerings of Daft.ie.

It has been a key strategy of management that the company continues to grow with the needs of its users. But another critical cornerstone of its success has been its ability to stay focused within the property market and not get diverted into activities that are outside its core strengths or knowledge. However, continuing to grow to meet user needs while not moving away from its key abilities may prove to be an increasingly difficult task to achieve.

CHALLENGES TO SUCCESS

While some observers may view Daft.ie's management approach as conservative, due to its twin policies of achieving growth through retained funding only and not committing to above-the-line advertising, the Fallon brothers view their approach as sensible organic growth. They point to their continued success among the rubble of the dot.com generation as proof that their methods have been successful to date. But even as the company continues to grow impressively from its modest beginnings, a number of key challenges still face the business.

The sustained growth of the company has meant that the Fallon brothers are no longer able to manage all of the activities of the business directly, and there is a strong need to delegate responsibilities among its staff. Indeed, an immediate task for the firm is to hire four new staff, but finding the right people for the position and the right fit for the company is proving difficult. Once the four people have been hired, they will then need to restructure the organisation, and current consideration is to departmentalise it along functional lines. While they are uncomfortable with this traditional structure, they are certain that they cannot run the day-to-day management of the business in the same way they have been doing since the foundation of the company. This growth in staff numbers will mean that the office space that the company currently uses will no longer be big enough to hold all of its employees. It has rented space at the Digital Hub for a number of years now and has enjoyed a very positive relationship with its landlord. Each time it needed to expand, office space has been found for its operations.

However, there may be no further room available for it and, while not wishing to leave, it may have no choice. The upheaval in moving to another location would also seriously disturb its focus on increasing revenue and profitability.

The threat from Internet businesses such as MyHome.ie and traditional businesses such as the Independent News and Media Group (owners of the *Evening Herald*) means that Daft.ie cannot afford to ignore the changing business environment. Management has identified the need to secure a very good salesperson, as sales are not happening as quickly as is needed to fund future plans. If sales do not increase significantly in the near future, then either the plans will have to be shelved or alternative sources of funding will have to be accessed. This latter option is not in keeping with a fundamental financial policy of the firm, and not developing the business activities of Daft.ie could lose it significant market share. However, the search for a good salesperson has proved difficult and the right person has yet to be located.

FUTURE OPPORTUNITIES

The areas of the business that provide greatest excitement for the Fallon brothers relate to future opportunities. The Fallons believe that, as with any business participating in the property market in Ireland, there are many wonderful possibilities to expand their operations. Interestingly, one of the strongest opportunities that they have identified is not within the Irish market but in the international arena. As a business model they have proven that Daft.ie works, so there is no reason why it cannot work equally well in other countries. They have considered franchising the business model, but would prefer not to take that option. Instead, they believe that they could run the operations for each country from Ireland, although they believe that each country would require its own locally based sales office. Such a move would also feed into another opportunity, which is to attract non-Irish investors into the Irish market. They see this as having enormous potential, although better value property deals can possibly now be found in eastern European countries. Another possibility within the same arena is to develop different language versions of Daft.ie, particularly for the Polish and Chinese markets, which have a substantial number of their people located in Ireland. However, the downside to this possibility is that it would require a full-time native speaker for each market to do the translations, and the return on investment through increased revenue would be poor.

Apart from these international opportunities, management believes that a significant number of possibilities to increase revenue continue to be available within its existing services, particularly through upselling to its current users. There are a large number of different types of markets, each with substantial potential customer numbers that have not yet been fully exploited. For example, commercial property was one of the fastest growing market segments in 2004, and yet the Daft.ie website does not push this area of its business offerings. Equally, parking spaces are available through the website but their revenue potential remains relatively untapped. Additionally, banner advertising is a considerable source of revenue for many Internet companies that innovatively utilise their space to create further income. While revenue from this activity has always featured strongly within Daft.ie, there undoubtedly remains significant potential for the company to increase its financial returns. Similarly, the recently developed mortgage centre is undersold and requires the attention of dedicated time to improve its revenue generation capacity. In fact, on reflection, at a recent management meeting the brothers agreed that all of the company's operations needed to be closely analysed to see how each area could have its financial potential maximised.

There was one other possibility recently discussed, although there is a combined reluctance to develop it further. Some other websites see themselves not simply as a property website but as a 'classifieds' website which also offers products such as jobs and cars. The positive aspect of this opportunity is that it greatly expands the customer base and the potential for revenue generation is substantial. The negative is that the company would no longer be focused in its operations and it would be copying traditional media. While neither brother had much enthusiasm for the idea, the potential opportunity that it offered meant that it could not be dismissed easily. It also opened up the discussion whereby diversifying its operations into other types of products beyond property was now being considered.

TIME TO BE INTERVIEWED

As the brothers discussed all of the issues and opportunities that the business faced, there was a knock on the office door and the reporter from

NewsTalk 106 was introduced to them. He had come to record an interview with them for the following week's edition of 'Down To Business'. Apparently the programme had been running a series over the previous six weeks dealing with different examples of good business practice, including:

- Listening to your customer.
- Constantly improving your product or service offering.
- Everyone in the organisation being responsible (for the customer, quality service, etc.).
- Exceeding expectations.
- Treating others as you would like to be treated.
- Focus, focus, focus.

As part of the series, listeners had been invited to nominate businesses that they believed best exemplified these principles, and Daft.ie had won the award. Without ever really setting out to deliberately implement these principles, the Fallons felt that their management style had allowed them to intuitively introduce them as the business grew. They always felt that they were primarily in business to help people, and that it was by doing this properly that they could be most successful. Their philosophy was obviously working so far, but would they be able to maintain these principles as they prepared to expand their business and move into new markets with new product offerings?

NOTES

1 This case was prepared by Dr Thomas M. Cooney as the basis for class discussion rather than to illustrate either effective or ineffective handling of a business situation.

2 Thomas Cooney is the Director of the Institute for Minority Entrepreneurship at Dublin Institute of Technology (Thomas.cooney@dit.ie). The author is extremely grateful to Eamonn and Brian Fallon for their time and their inspiration in helping to prepare this case.

3 ABC Electronic (2006) 'Daft.ie Now Ireland's Busiest Certified Property Site', *ABC Electronic*, available at: <http://www.abce.org.uk/cgi-bin/gen5?runprog=abce/abce &type=page&p=news_200706.html&menuid=news%7Cn1%7Cnews_200706%7C news_200706> [accessed 27 July 2007].

Exhibit 1
Audience Figures (ABC Certified*)

	Total	Daily Averages
Page Impressions	27,675,927	892,772
Unique Users	425,149	24,047

*Total qualifying traffic for the certification period 1 May–31 May 2006
Source: ABC ELECTRONIC 2006

Exhibit 2
Top Irish ABC Audited Websites

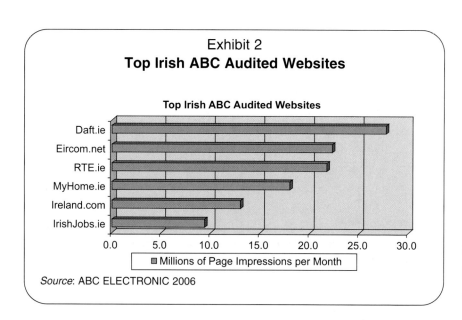

Top Irish ABC Audited Websites

■ Millions of Page Impressions per Month

Source: ABC ELECTRONIC 2006

Martin McKay
Texthelp Systems[1]

LORNA TREANOR[2]

INTRODUCTION

In a former nylon factory in a modest industrial estate in Antrim, Martin McKay sits in his office at the international HQ of Texthelp Systems. He is contemplating how he can further push the barriers of assistive technology. As Technical Director and founding entrepreneur of Texthelp, to Martin McKay "it can't be done" simply means, "it just hasn't been done yet". In fact, this 36-year-old has revolutionised life for millions of people since founding Texthelp in 1996 through his innovative software which, among other things, allows books to read themselves to you whilst you read along with the text, or allows you to access a version of your tax return form online that will pronounce the words you have difficulty with, so you can complete it yourself, embarrassment free. The passion and focus that delivered these technological advances have driven Texthelp Systems to become a market leader in the UK and number two in the American market. Ten years ago Martin McKay risked the family farm to establish this company and bring his product to market; today this same company is valued at $40–50 million. The question now facing Martin is how does he continue to meet the needs of his customers while maximising the value of this company for his other shareholders?

COMPANY BACKGROUND – THE FORMATION OF TEXTHELP SYSTEMS

He was a 23-year-old but, as Martin McKay, says:

> I was confident, not only in my technical ability, but also in my ability to 'nouse out' a good money-making opportunity;

> after all, I had been doing that since I was ten. There was
> no plan B, having a plan B would be like planning to fail.
> I was pig-headed and I knew what I wanted to do.[3]

Martin established a multimedia business, operating as a sole trader. Despite his inexperience, he made a bid for a STG£250,000 contract with the Northern Bank who, somewhat nervous about its investment, advised him to partner with an older and more experienced firm. Although his business was performing well, even then Martin knew it was not scalable and would never generate the financial return he sought. Therefore Martin invested and became a partner in Lorien Systems, a business located in the offices Texthelp Systems calls home today.

During his early time with Lorien Systems, Martin was demonstrating a multimedia product in Altnagelvin Hospital. A speech therapist in attendance at the demonstration mentioned the potential to use that technology in their field. Martin later pursued this with a visit to the speech therapy unit to gain a better understanding of their needs and to see at first-hand the technologies being employed.

> The technology they were using was really very basic and
> I thought – we could do better than that!

Martin developed prototypes of new technological solutions which, following demonstration, were purchased by Altnagelvin Hospital. This was the start of a journey into "assistive technology" that would result in the establishment and growth of Texthelp Systems. "Assistive technology" refers to any aid or technology that helps people to undertake daily activities. It can range from a walking stick to facilitate mobility, to specialised hardware such as electronic, computerised wheelchairs, through to software such as that developed by Texthelp Systems.

While providing solutions to universities to promote access for students with cerebral palsy, MS and similar conditions, Martin realised that dyslexia amongst students was a major problem. Once again, through developing relationships with his customers, he was able to identify market opportunities by providing solutions to meet customer needs. Martin did his homework. While 0.05 per cent of the population suffered from cerebral palsy and could use his existing assistive technology, 7 per cent had dyslexia and 19 per cent experienced literacy difficulties. Martin immediately recognised the scale of the problem and the scale of the opportunity; 19 per cent of any market is a significant market. If he changed focus and developed a new product for this target group then his market size would increase 300 fold!

Having spent two years researching the subject and travelling to California to meet experts in the field, Martin developed software technologies to respond to these identified needs. He raised STG£100,000 to fund his developmental work by using some of his father's land as a security, but this was not going to be enough to drive this product and business to achieve its full potential. Venture capital (VC) funding was necessary. At this stage, Martin McKay was 25 years old.

In 1996, a venture capital company interested in young, high potential, technology-based companies in Ireland and the UK decided to invest in a young, dynamic entrepreneur with a good product; Texthelp Systems was created. Unusually, Martin's shareholding increased during the VC period, and he is now the largest shareholder in the business. At the end of the first year following VC funding, the previous MD left the company. Martin was offered and declined the CEO position. He recognised that this was not where his interest or his strengths lay; he wanted to continue as Technical Director, developing the technology, motivating his teams and pushing the business forward. An interim MD was brought in, who turned out to be a very beneficial mentor to Martin. He offered good practical advice, telling him, "never let your resources impact upon your decision-making", toughening him up and helping him to make unpleasant business decisions. The venture capital investment company sourced a Managing Director who was brought in seven years ago on a deal that allowed him to gain a significant shareholding. Texthelp Systems was now firmly established and set for growth.

Despite this success, Martin does not regard himself as an entrepreneur:

> I haven't really done anything yet. Entrepreneurs are individuals who are audacious in business; I haven't built anything of scale yet, but I'm getting there.

He cites Richard Branson, as well as some lesser-known examples of "real entrepreneurs". Martin considers his time in Texthelp Systems as an apprenticeship; when his involvement with the company comes to an end, he will probably start another business that would be completely different and enable him to work outdoors, as he dislikes being based in an office.

His advice to anyone thinking about starting up on their own is to "do it! Pay no heed to the nay-sayers." Unperturbed by the negativity and criticism from others which has characterised his business life from start-up, Martin McKay portrays hard work, determination and unfailing creativity. He warns that the only thing new entrepreneurs need be careful of is employing people:

> If your business fails and you work alone, you go hungry – if your business fails and you have staff, families go hungry! I would also advise anyone considering venture capital to seek good legal advice, as well as advice from someone who has already accessed VC funding.

THE CHILD MAKETH THE MAN

Two experiences of twelve-year-old Martin McKay have had a strong influence on the man who sits as Technical Director and founding entrepreneur of Texthelp Systems today. Martin remembers standing with a runny nose in a wet field in the freezing cold, he was twelve years old and "snedding" turnips was an unpleasant job that day:

> I remember the boss – the man who owned the field and paid the wages – driving up in his big car to check up on everything, before driving off again. I thought "it's much better being the owner than being the worker and making someone else rich!"

Martin had several role models for self-employment. He recalls that everyone he knew, his dad and all his uncles, were self-employed. Although he did not know exactly what he wanted to do when he was older, twelve-year-old Martin McKay knew he wanted to be his own boss.

It was at this age too that Martin's father had a stroke and was, for a time, severely disabled, unable to speak and partially paralysed. Martin helped his other family members to teach his dad to speak again using flashcards – reinforcing the word by enabling his father to see it and hear it at the same time. This is the same technique now deployed by his *Read and Write* product in an electronic format to help people with cognitive disabilities or poor vision to read.

Martin is the second of four children and the eldest boy. Martin's father told him he could have anything he wanted so long as he paid for half of it himself. Young Martin could not believe his luck. "The whole world was on 50 per cent sale!" he recalls, "I just had to work to get whatever I wanted." Martin remembers always working hard from a young age. At age ten he picked strawberries for cash, at twelve he was "snedding" turnips and at thirteen or fourteen he was paid STG£4 for every 1,000 cabbages he planted. This was good training for later years when Martin worked fourteen-hour days, seven days per week for five years, whilst developing his products and establishing his business.

Growing up on a farm that was too small to give work to two boys, Martin knew from the age of fifteen that he had to make his living from something other than farming. Having spent some time reading Agricultural Microbiology at Queen's University Belfast, Martin quickly found this subject not to his liking and applied to change to a computing course. Computers captured his interest and, with multimedia being in its infancy at that time, he recognised the significant potential and opportunities in this area. Having taken a year out to gain appropriate A-Levels in Physics and Computing, Martin commenced his degree in Computer Science. At the end of the second year of his course, Martin went to his tutor and told him he was withdrawing from his degree course to go and start his own business.

> I already knew enough to do me by then and I would not
> have learned very much more in that last year anyway. So
> I thought I'd just get out there, get started straight away
> and get on with it, rather than waiting another year before
> doing it.

Of course his tutor advised him not to proceed with this madness but to stay and complete his degree course so he would "have something to fall back on".

PRODUCT RANGE

Simply put, Texthelp Systems produces products that help people to read – those people can be university students, primary or secondary school pupils, or adults at home, in the workplace or on the web. Its technologies include Talking Textbooks, Talking Websites, Talking Dictionaries and Spellcheckers.

Since it was formed in 1996, Texthelp Systems has become the global market leader in assistive technology to help literacy in education. Undoubtedly, the political and social landscape of the past decade, particularly with human rights issues becoming entrenched in legislation, has helped this company to maximise the potential of its products. In Britain, every child has the right to an education and similar policy developments are occurring in the USA with the "No Child Left Behind" campaign.

Texthelp's initial box-product offering was its Dyslexia solution – *Read and Write Gold*.[4] This flagship product was widely acclaimed and won "Best Instructional Solution: Special Needs Students" in the internationally renowned Software and Information Industry Association's Annual CODiE[5] Awards. The software records changes in the user's ability, tracks progress and enables teachers to identify the particular area where each individual has difficulty, e.g. homonyms, spelling, etc. This information is also fed back to Texthelp Systems for marketing and research purposes (see Exhibit 1).

Consistent growth, focused management and constant innovation have allowed this company to expand through diversifying into new markets, namely e-Government[6] and educational publishing.

Browsealoud[7] is a spin-off technology that introduces text-to-speech into e-Government, increasing accessibility. The Speech Services Business Unit of Texthelp responsible for the *Browsealoud* product was established in the UK in 2003 as a separate business unit with its own independent profit and loss accounts. Today, over 30 per cent of UK local government has signed up as a *Browsealoud* customer; this means end-users can download the software free of charge in order to complete forms or access information. The 2005/2006 financial year saw *Browsealoud* generate STG£1 million revenue in the UK market, and the product is still in the introduction phase of its product life cycle.

Browsealoud is a patented technology and is to be formally launched in the USA this year. Full-time sales and marketing staff are already in place, and the product is expected to generate $250,000 in its first year, as Martin explains:

> Year One is an awareness-raising year. The company must
> get the marketing message fine-tuned and disseminated

appropriately before investing significant finance to establish it in the US market. Year Two will be the growth year through the implementation of a strong sales strategy and that's when we will start to see real money coming in.

Texthelp has now transitioned its box product software into the educational publishing market. The educational publishing industry represents a significant global market with an annual turnover in the region of STG£20 billion. Whilst there are six large companies that dominate the educational publishing market, no single provider currently dominates the educational software market sector. This offers great scope for an ambitious, innovative and responsive company to carve out a sizeable niche.

As a first foray into this market Texthelp has released three Talking Textbooks in California; its American client (who provides the content) expects to increase sales of its "Middle School[8] Maths" book by over $3 million as a result of providing the book in the speaking format. The potential across the series of books covering the school curricula for all age ranges is huge.

The educational publishing market promises to be very lucrative for Texthelp shareholders. However this is an industry that is typified by buy-outs, takeovers and amalgamations. If Texthelp and its market offerings are strategically developed to suit this sector a corporate purchase of Texthelp Systems in the future, by a large educational publishing company, may not be beyond the realms of possibility. However, Martin seems determined to establish Texthelp within this market and to, again, take on the competition and beat them in their own backyard.

Market Penetration

Due to the often limited income of its end-user group, Texthelp has developed its business by targeting the educational providers and, latterly, government departments, who have large budgets and a responsibility to provide an education or information/access to the target user group. The ability to have large-order customers has meant that the company could grow quickly and offer its solutions at affordable prices for individual end users. In order to develop and provide such innovative solutions at affordable prices the company had two options – either enter new markets or increase the price. Instead, it did both and "it worked quite well". Texthelp also offer parents whose children attend schools with site licenses half-price software for use at home.

The UK and American markets are vastly different and thus different approaches were taken in selling the educational software solutions. The UK is a smaller market, meaning that a channel-focused approach would enable this market to be easily managed by a small number of people. Texthelp set out to recruit fifty resellers, based on the assumption that ten of those would be good and worth retaining. As it turned out, however, ten were very good and fifteen are good, so the company has twenty-five resellers throughout the UK. The centralised decision-making systems in the UK also facilitated market access and penetration, as centralised funding schemes meant that the company could influence grant schemes through marketing and product demonstrations. The company employs around forty-five people in Northern Ireland and is currently hiring additional sales staff.

In comparison the US market is geographically vast and disparate with state-based decision-making. Unlike the UK market, grants are provided on an individual basis through Individual Education Plans (IEPs). Resellers tend to comprise of affected families in this market, as opposed to growth-oriented sales companies, so this was not considered the appropriate path to market for the US. A more direct approach was required; in order to acquire big sales, statewide tender contracts were the target.

There were three or four major competitors operating in the educational software market at this time and Texthelp was regarded as a "no-hoper" market entry, since it had no presence in the market, no understanding of American culture and its expectation that people would phone Northern Ireland for technical support was regarded as "crazy". However, persistence and the company's approach, i.e. listening to customers, responding to customers and letting them know you have responded to them, won it business.

Texthelp now has fifteen staff in the US, half of which are sales staff. It is now number two in the market, with the company valued in the region of $40–50 million and stealing market share quite rapidly. Texthelp Systems anticipate being market leader in two years time.

THE MARKETS

Currently, Texthelp Systems can be regarded as straddling two markets – the assistive technology market and the educational publishing market.

Although the company develops assistive technology, it does so primarily for application in the educational markets. This offers the opportunity to strategically develop the company to position it firmly in the educational publishing market as an attractive subsidiary purchase for a large publishing company such as Pearson to acquire. This decision must be made in light of the following market information:

The European assistive technology market is worth over €30 billion (just over £20 billion sterling). However, due to different national policies on reimbursement and differing political objectives, there is often a focus on individual impairments and needs. For this reason, there are no large players and the market is dominated by SMEs (small to medium-sized enterprises).[9] Microsoft commissioned Forrester Research to examine the nature and potential of the market for computer-related assistive technology (AT) in the United States. This research report[10] found that 37 per cent of US adults aged eighteen and over had mild difficulties that would mean they would be "likely to benefit" from such AT, with 25 per cent having severe difficulties and being "very likely to benefit" from applications similar to those market offerings belonging to Texthelp Systems. The research then concentrated on those likely or very likely to benefit from this assistance (see Exhibit 2).

The market for Texthelp Systems' *Read and Write* is significant, with 33.5 million adults having a cognitive disability. Add to this the numbers with visual difficulties and those who are learning in their second language and you can start to see the potential for this product that has yet to be realised in this marketplace.

In terms of future market potential, the Forrester Study reported that:

> By 2020, one in five workers will be 55 years and older. This represents a more than 50% increase over 2000, in which 13% of the labor force was made up of the 55-and-older age group. The aging labor force is likely to mean greater pressure from businesses to help keep their aging employees as productive as possible throughout their careers[11].... (Moreover)... Aging brings about the need for accessible technology in two ways. First, as people age, existing mild difficulties and impairments can become more severe. Second, people are likely to develop new difficulties and impairments as they age. In a population in which the age profile is shifting rapidly

toward those most likely to have difficulties and impairments, the total number of people with difficulties and
impairments will increase.[12]

The alternative is to establish the company in the educational publishing
market. In the UK, Key Note's Publishing Market review for 2006[13]
reports that the UK publishing industry alone was worth STG£18.63 billion
(around €28 billion) in 2005, having increased by 7.5 per cent across the
period from 2001 to 2005. The report estimates an 8.8 per cent growth
between 2006 and 2010.

In the USA, a recent market research report cites Pearson as the top
educational publishing company.[14] This same report also anticipates a
3–4 per cent market growth through 2008. The market value of textbooks
sold into the college market alone in 2004 was $5.57 billion (around
€4.22 billion or STG£2.84 billion). This report highlighted that electronic
books were "receiving a cool reception on the college campuses".
However industry reports widely recognised the digitisation of books and
electronic media as being a key challenge and, by default, a huge opportunity for the educational publishing industries globally. This is also a
market sector where acquisition is commonplace.

KEY SUCCESS FACTORS

Innovation is at the heart of Texthelp Systems operations – twenty-five of
the company's sixty staff are employed in research and development
(R&D). The technical advancements are underpinned by research and
development activity that is consistently ongoing. Texthelp retain very
close links with the research community; it has an ongoing research plan
with Queen's University Belfast, which has just completed a two-year
study. A two-year study is also ongoing in Kentucky and an article on
Texthelp's products and the improvement in reading ability as a result has
just been published in the *Journal of Special Education Technology*. At any
one time there are at least two two-year research studies ongoing. The data
gathered from products such as *Read and Write* and *Browsealoud* feed into
this research, which in turn underpins future developments with the products and product ranges. Martin states that this research activity is under-
taken primarily to support sales, so that Texthelp can prove to customers
that its products actually improve an individual's ability to read and write.

All innovation in the company is driven from the top but is market-led. The company keeps a close eye on market trends and patterns; by knowing and listening to its customers Texthelp has come to dominate its market. In 1999, the most popular name for newborn boys in California was John; in 2002 it was José. In four years the majority of the population in this market will be of Hispanic origin, meaning that they are learning in their second language. 70 per cent of children read below their grade level in the American market, and 40 per cent read two levels below their grade level. The American government realises that this is a social problem and has introduced a "No Child Left Behind" policy. Martin McKay sees Texthelp as offering the solutions to address these social problems. These trends and emerging patterns are now shaping the sales strategies for 2008–2010, and recruitment for sales staff is currently ongoing.

A key reason for the success of Texthelp's assistive technology products is the fact that the company constantly listens to its customers and keeps closely in tune with its markets. In the USA it has established a special advisory group comprising educational psychology experts from universities and two exceptional student education directors,[15] amongst others. The focus-group days are divided into two sections: the morning focuses on critical feedback on products from the foregoing year, and the afternoon is used to demonstrate prototypes and gather feedback on desirable features and relevance to user needs. This not only fosters ownership amongst key purchase decision-makers within their key markets, but it also provides useful feedback to aid product enhancements before introduction to the market.

Staff training and development is another key contributor to Texthelp Systems' success. When you enter the reception area of Texthelp's offices, you cannot fail to notice the company's training and development policy to the fore of the company noticeboard. Above it is the quality policy; below it the mission statement – "To provide high quality and innovative assistive technology for any person of any age seeking to develop their language skills through the use of a computer" – and surrounding them are the obligatory Health and Safety and insurance notices.

By today's strict company standards, neither Martin nor the current MD would be eligible for employment with Texthelp Systems – to be employed in R&D, individuals must be honours graduates with a minimum of four years' experience. In return, Texthelp Systems strives to offer staff a challenging and rewarding environment that will not stifle their creativity, in addition to good remuneration packages and training and development opportunities. The fact that they work for a socially responsible company and that the staff use their skills to help others are also factors likely to contribute to the low staff turnover rates enjoyed by the company. Martin says the only acceptable reason for someone wanting to leave his company is to go and start their own business. If they are unhappy, de-motivated or not getting paid satisfactorily, then he has not done his job properly. As a result, Texthelp Systems has a team who constantly strive to improve and innovate to deliver new and better assistive technology solutions.

The technology for *Browsealoud* was developed two years before it was market feasible, as customers did not have the bandwidth to support the technology used. However, Martin was sure there was a market for the product, even though his Board were not as convinced. Despite thinking Martin was "crazy" for considering the development of the *Browsealoud* product (their two main US competitors had both tried, failed and abandoned the development of this product) he managed to convince them that they could develop the technology and successfully bring it to market. That was easier to do then, as the Board comprised a smaller number of people to persuade. Martin seems to fear Texthelp Systems becoming like its competitors, too rigid and unresponsive, meaning that a good idea cannot be pursued because the metrics of the project "don't seem to fit".

A recent introduction to the market was a pen drive or memory stick, which contains the assistive software, meaning that someone with dyslexia or other reading difficulty can use any PC and still use the *Browsealoud* product whilst online. The company has five patents lodged. Due to the nature of the software industry the intention is to dissuade others from copying its products; however Martin is aware that "there are many different ways of arriving at the one destination in computer programming".

Martin is making plans today for the introduction of another new technological advancement that he will bring to the market in two years' time.

FUTURE PLANS

Texthelp currently has an online education product in the very early stages of development. It is planned to have a prototype of this software ready to demonstrate in Miami and Fort Lauderdale (the two largest educational areas in the US) during the summer of 2007. The feedback from this pilot and from its advisory groups will be incorporated into the revised iteration of the software, prior to the establishment of another independent business unit built around this product.

Concurrent development of the existing business streams will be ongoing to ensure a continued straight-line growth of revenue and profit for the company that will make it increasingly attractive and more valuable to potential purchasers. The company routinely measures its EBITDA (Earnings Before Interest Taxes Depreciation and Amortisation), i.e. its value if it were to be sold. All companies are required to measure this value and submit it annually to Companies House as part of their annual reports. Texthelp's EBITDA has continually increased and Martin is focused on ensuring continued growth to maximise returns for shareholders.

Martin McKay aims to open a new Texthelp Systems Business Unit every two years as a means of ensuring continued straight-line growth in the company's revenue. The strategy employed to maintain this straight-line growth is to overlap the introduction and growth stages of each concurrent product and business life cycle to result in a net straight-line growth for Texthelp Systems as a whole (see Exhibit 3).

The challenge, therefore, is twofold. Martin must first ensure that the company is positioned in the correct marketplace, with the company holding sizeable market share and innovative technological solutions that will ensure its attractiveness and value to a prospective customer. Secondly, in the process of doing this, Martin needs to ensure that the company (and larger Board) does not become so engrossed in measurements and metrics that it becomes unresponsive to market opportunities and threats, just like its competitors were in relation to Texthelp itself and its innovative products.

Texthelp Systems is probably entering its most challenging phase, where Martin has to find a path that will enable consolidation without encouraging complacency or stagnancy, yet facilitate innovation and growth without incurring too much risk. It is imperative to position the company within the correct market and facilitate continued growth, to maximise return on investment from acquisition. Texthelp Systems must decide whether to position itself in the assistive technology market or to develop new products to support a strong position in the educational publishing market. This strategic decision, and the supporting marketing strategy that will be developed along with it, will prove crucial at Martin McKay's exit stage of Texthelp Systems' business life cycle. As I leave Martin McKay to consider how he is going to continue to meet the needs of his customers and his need to push the technological barriers, whilst also positioning his company and maximising its value to enhance the prospects of a lucrative sale, I have no doubt he will succeed in meeting his goals.

NOTES

1 This case was prepared by Lorna Treanor as the basis for class discussion rather than to illustrate either effective or ineffective handling of a business situation.

2 Lorna Treanor is Research Supervisor in the Centre for Entrepreneurship Research at Dundalk Institute of Technology (lorna.treanor@dkit.ie). The author is extremely grateful to Martin McKay for his time and inspiration in helping to prepare this case.

3 Interview with Martin McKay on 8 November 2006. All other quotations from Martin McKay in this case are from the same interview.

4 The *Read and Write* product is an additional toolbar that enables the user to highlight words and have them read back to them, even the spell-checker and calculator have read-back. It provides help with homophones, monitors the user's writing style and predicts words they are looking for. This software also offers alternative solutions to broaden vocabulary. Teachers can be provided with reports to identify particular weaknesses and improvements.

5 CODiE awards are annual awards made by the Software and Information Industry Association for "Excellence in Software Development".

6 E-Government is a contraction of "electronic government". It is the utilisation of electronic technology to streamline or otherwise improve the business of government, oftentimes with respect to exchanging services and information with citizens, businesses and other arms of government. (Wikipedia (2006), available at: <http://en.wikipedia.org/wiki/E-Government> [accessed 14 December 2006]).

7 The *Browsealoud* product reads webpages aloud for people with difficulty reading, with literacy difficulties or for whom English is a second language.

8 Middle school refers to Grades 6 to 8 in the American secondary school system, equivalent to first through third year of the UK and Irish secondary school sytems.

9 According to Prof. Ing Christian Buhler, President of the Association for the Advancement of Assistive Technology in Europe (AAATE) 2000.

10 Forrester Research (2003), 'The Wide Range of Abilities and Its Impact on Computer Technology', available at: <http://www.microsoft.com/enable/research/default.aspx> [accessed 14 December 2006].

11 Forrester Research, 2003, p. 13.

12 Forrester Research, 2003, p. 14.

13 Key Note (2006) 'The Publishing Industry Marketing Review 2006', available at: <http://www.researchandmarkets.com/reportinfo.asp?report_id=340227> [accessed 14 December 2006].

14 Simba Information Inc. (July 2005), 'College Publishing Market Forecast 2005–2006'.

15 "Exceptional Students" is the American terminology for the Irish and UK equivalent term "Special Needs" children. Each state has a Director of Education for Exceptional Students responsible for commissioning services and products to meet the educational needs of this student group.

Exhibit 1
Read and Write Product and Users

The *Read and Write* Product in its packaging and as it appears on the user's screen.

The Floating Toolbar

Spelling Help

Read and Write Users

Exhibit 2
Likelihood to Benefit from the Use of Accessible Technology According to Type of Difficulty or Impairment among Working-Age Adults

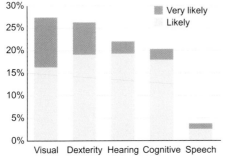

	Likely (millions)	Very likely (millions)	Total
Visual	27.4	18.5	45.9
Dexterity	31.7	12.0	43.7
Hearing	32.0	4.3	36.3
Cognitive	29.7	3.8	33.5
Speech	4.3	1.9	6.2

Base: US 18- to 64-year-olds

Source: Study commissioned by Microsoft, conducted by Forrester Research, Inc, 2003.

Exhibit 3
Business Life Cycle

www.valuebasedmanagement.net

Product (Industry) Life Cycle Stages

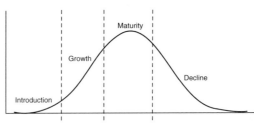

Last accessed on 16 February 2007 at:
<http://www.valuebasedmanagement.net/methods_product_life_cycle.html>

Joanna Gardiner Ovelle Pharmaceuticals[1]

Colette Henry[2]

Introduction

Sitting in her office on the Coes Road, Dundalk, Ovelle's newly appointed Managing Director is brimming with enthusiasm for the pharmaceutical business that her grandparents had established some seventy years previous. She has just signed off on a series of quirky radio ads using the 'Save your Skin' slogan, designed to boost brand awareness on a national level. She has, by all accounts, already turned what was a small, family-run and, according to some, floundering company into a highly competitive, growth-oriented venture, widely respected within the skincare market. After all, Ovelle's Elave® range of irritant-free body washes, shampoos and intensive creams is now a well-established brand in the marketplace. However, for this young, dynamic Trinity graduate, the biggest challenge is yet to come. Having, by her own admission, taken the company "by the scruff of the neck" and made "really tough business decisions along the way", Joanna is gearing up to lead Ovelle through a major expansion phase which will extend its export sales to the global market – a market controlled by just a handful of multi-national companies. From a marketing perspective, the time is right – the general toiletries market, within which the skincare market is categorised, is forecast to grow by some 16 per cent over the next five years. But competing at *the global level* will inevitably mean more changes within the company: significant further investment, a new recruitment drive and an international marketing campaign. This will undoubtedly present Joanna with another exciting challenge, fuelling her marketing drive as well as her passion for advertising. Thinking about her small team of just fifty staff and the tough decisions she had to make in the recent shake-up, Joanna can't help but ask herself the question – is Ovelle ready for another major restructuring?

COMPANY BACKGROUND

When you walk into Ovelle Pharmaceuticals the first thing that strikes you is its compliance with industry standards. The reception walls are filled with quality certificates issued from the recognised national and international authorities – evidence that the company meets the highest technical standards in terms of both product and process. The commitment to its staff is also evident, with a range of Excellence through People awards hanging on the reception walls alongside various other export and environmental awards.

Founded in 1934, Ovelle Pharmaceuticals is a privately owned family business based in Dundalk, Co. Louth, Ireland. The company has always been viewed as a small owner-managed business, manufacturing old-fashioned, unbranded traditional creams and lotions, such as calamine lotion, Silcock's Base and emulsifying ointments. Such products were typically sold over the counter by pharmacists all over the country and were highly regarded by GPs.

Joanna only became involved in the business in 2000, when the company was, for the most part, seen as small and static, content to continue servicing its existing markets without deliberate expansion. Joanna's role at that point had been mainly marketing and promotion, a role she envisaged retaining for the foreseeable future. However, shortly after Joanna joined the company, Ovelle underwent a major restructuring. Staffing levels were reduced and a strategy was developed to refocus the business as a sales-led organisation. To fund the planned restructuring, two local private investors were secured, in addition to funding from Enterprise Ireland.[3] This resulted in the company moving from a family-owned business run by her father, Sean Gardiner, to a company with significant external shareholding. Joanna played a major role in the restructuring process and, in 2002, was appointed Managing Director.

Under Joanna's direction, Ovelle's new challenges would include growing the export business and introducing a branded skincare product line. With an increase in skin complaints such as eczema, psoriasis and dry skin, Joanna saw an opportunity to produce irritant-free pharmaceutical products that were not damaging to the skin. The resulting Elave (formerly Emulave) brand would be more consumer-friendly, taking less time and effort to administer, yet it would deliver the same benefits as the company's existing product line. Another key challenge would involve bringing the company from a turnover of around €2m with a loss of €0.3m, to a profitable, growth-oriented operation.

OVELLE'S PRODUCT RANGE

Ovelle's core competency is the formulation, development and production of dermatological, pharmaceutical and healthcare products. Fully licensed by the Irish Medicines Board (IMB) to manufacture multi-dose liquid, semi-solid and solid pharmaceuticals, Ovelle's manufacturing permit is recognised in all EU countries and by the World Health Organisation. Its product range includes emollients, antiseptics, muscle and skin treatments, coal tar preparation and sun blocks for the domestic and export market, which it supplies to pharmaceutical wholesalers, pharmacy chains and independents.

Ovelle operate the Quality Assurance Standards (QAS) and Good Manufacturing Practice (GMP) in its production processes – internationally recognised standards for the pharmaceutical industry. Its manufacturing license requires quality assurance of the highest standards, typically in excess of ISO9000 and the Q Mark. As a result, Ovelle are in the envious position of being registered suppliers for the United Nations and the United Nations Children's Fund, and carry out contract manufacturing on behalf of aid agencies worldwide.

The company's key brand – Elave – is a range of irritant-free body washes, shampoos, lotions, oils, facial cleansers and intensive creams (see Exhibit 1). These products contain no alcohol, soap, colouring dye, perfume, parabens or formaldehyde. Sales of the Elave range have grown dramatically over the past three years, making it the number one brand in the Irish skin care market for dermatology products, ahead of its key competitor E45. Highly recommended by pharmacists, dermatologists and GPs for the treatment of a wide range of skin conditions, Elave products are now sold nationwide in selected multiples, including Boots, McCabe's and McCauley's retail pharmacy chains, as well as in some of the Dunnes Stores, Tesco and Superquinn outlets. In addition, Elave products have just recently become available online (<http://www.elave.ie>), adding a significant new dimension to Ovelle's sales strategy and its turnover.

The Competition and Industry Trends

As mentioned above, Ovelle's biggest competitor product is E45, a range that consists of products specially formulated for people with dry skin. All E45 products are perfume-free and its washing products contain no soaps or detergents. Like the Elave range, E45 products have been dermatologically tested and endorsed by healthcare professionals (<http://www.E45.com>). However, the exact make up of the competition depends very much on your particular perspective, i.e. what market is Ovelle actually in? In the strictest sense, Ovelle is firmly grounded in the skincare market, more specifically, within the dry-skin and dermatological market. But these days the lines between dermatological and cosmetic skincare products are more than just slightly blurred, with the crossover from one market to the other becoming increasingly evident in media coverage, market reports and industry statistics.

Since the mid 1990s, individuals worldwide have been spending more per capita on skincare than ever before. The trend towards better skincare is set to continue, with European and Japanese consumers showing even greater awareness of the retail skincare market than in the United States.[4] Today, the consumer skincare market includes a vast array of anti-aging products, anti-fungals, moisturisers, medicated shampoos, body washes, lotions, oils, facial cleansers, intensive anti-irritant creams and sun-care products.

However, accurate data for the skincare market is difficult to come by, with not all over-the-counter sales being tracked and marketing reports typically categorising skincare products within the more general toiletries industry, which tends to overlap with the cosmetics industry. In the USA, for example, the skincare market witnessed a compound annual growth rate of 14.5 per cent between 1995 and 2000 (see Exhibit 2). In the UK the toiletries industry, which is led by multinationals Unilever and Procter & Gamble, grew by 3.3 per cent in 1999 to around STG£3.42 billion. Current forecasts indicate that the sector will continue to grow by more than 16 per cent between 2005 and 2009.[5]

The reasons for the phenomenal growth of the skincare market can be explained in part by the industry's improved access to research and technology on a global scale, better scientific testing facilities, greater consumer awareness of skincare (including being better educated about the potential skin damage caused by the sun and other environmental effects, as well as being able to recognise potentially harmful chemical ingredients), and an increase in Internet shopping. Furthermore, the industry has been quick to note that skincare consumers are loyal customers who tend to stick with their chosen brand, something that is not typically seen in cosmetics, its sister industry.

According to the *New York Times*, today's skincare companies are marrying science to mass customisation, but this scientific approach comes at a price, with consumers witnessing as much as a 100 per cent price increase on some of the traditional leading brands, such as Olay or Neutrogena. Visually attractive packages that carry labels with complex formulae and high tech–sounding ingredients promising to 'reduce', 'diminish' and 'protect' are not without their critics:

> [T]hey talk about some high-tech sounding protein that slows the aging process ... but very few ingredients do the things they say they do, and I'm not sure all of them are safe (Dr Leslie Baumann, University of Miami School of Medicine[6]).

Notwithstanding the above, on a purely commercial level the scientific marketing approach would appear to be working:

> The plethora of molecules du jour was probably inevitable. More than a decade ago, companies began putting alpha hydroxy acids, retinols and retinoids, vitamins C and E, and all kinds of other scientific ingredients into what used to be mundane creams. Their sales shot up.[7]

However, in contrast to the scientific approach, there is also evidence of an underlying trend towards natural ingredients, with an interest in herbal derivatives and an increased awareness of potentially harmful chemical ingredients (see Exhibit 3). Indeed, in recent years critics of the skincare industry have been quick to alert consumers to the staggering proliferation of toxic chemicals appearing in everyday personal care products. The long-term safety of continued exposure to chemicals such as propylene glycol (PG) – used in toothpastes and aftershaves, polyethylene glycol (PEG) – found in most skin cleansers, isopropyl and alcohol – found in body rubs and hand lotions, sodium lauryl sulphate (SLS) – a foaming ingredient found in toothpastes and bubble baths, and formaldehyde – used in moisturisers and shampoos – is now becoming a key concern for consumers. It is claimed that such harmful and toxic chemicals not only contribute to the development of skin complaints such as asthma and eczema, but that they can also cause much more serious conditions such as Crohn's disease, IBS, ME, MS or cancer.[8]

Back at Ovelle, Joanna Gardiner is all too aware of the resulting confusion in the market place, but sees a clear opportunity for her product range:

> These days consumers are more educated about good skincare, and are not just buying to treat skin complaints such as eczema, psoriasis or dry skin; rather they are buying to protect their skin. They are much more conscious of the dangers of long-term exposure to chemical-based ingredients that appear in so many everyday skin products. The time has come to cater for the 'worried well', not just those with actual skin complaints.

THE MAKING OF AN ENTREPRENEUR

Personal Background

The mother of three children – a girl and two boys (aged ten, eight and three years respectively) – Joanna grew up in Dundalk and attended the local Louis School. Her parents were pharmacists but Joanna never considered herself to be a scientist. "I never really liked science subjects at school", she admits, "I just ended up studying Physics and Science because I was told to – it seemed to make sense at the time". At university she picked business-type subjects, which seemed to suit her well. As Joanna puts it, "at least with Business I didn't have to struggle with complex scientific formulae".

Joanna graduated from Trinity College Dublin (TCD) with a degree in Business and Politics in the early 1990s when there were virtually no jobs. At that time, there were many State-funded programmes available to provide fresh graduates with much-needed work experience. However, the average salary on these schemes was around IR£12,000, prompting most graduates to head for London or further afield in search of work. Joanna managed to get a marketing placement with an engineering company, where her job involved developing a marketing image for the business. She quickly made the company realise that it was not capitalising on its product offering and was, as she put it, "giving an awful lot away for free". While this placement worked out well, Joanna's real interest was in advertising. She had always loved watching the ad campaigns on TV and her passion eventually landed her a job as an account executive in design with the Helm Partnership in Dublin. The range of both products and clients that she encountered gave her valuable experience of different markets – she just loved advertising. She became really impressed with the entrepreneurial and management style of the company's managing director, Donald Helm. She admired his interpersonal skills, his creativity and the way he worked with his clients. In particular, she noted how he often took time out to just think things through before making decisions.

> I used to come in to his office and he would be just sitting there and it looked like he was doing nothing. But after a while he would start to write or get on the phone or call us together to outline a new idea. I really admired his approach. That's the problem with business today – we don't seem to take time out to just think.

The Decision to Join Ovelle

Despite her obvious passion for her work, on a personal level Joanna was going through a difficult time. Living in Dublin with (then) two children was not easy and, apart from the obvious stresses of city life, appropriate childcare was hard to find. So, in 1999, Joanna moved back to Dundalk in search of a better quality of life for both herself and her children. Her parents were based in Dundalk and this sense of family was important to her. Soon, she began working for the family business as Marketing Manager.

At that point Sean Gardiner, Joanna's father – the company's Managing Director – had just developed a dermatological wash product, Elave. Joanna saw immediate value in the product. As a mother who often took her children swimming, she had witnessed first-hand the difficulties that other mothers encountered as they tried to administer the traditional heavy-duty lotions to children suffering from skin complaints such as eczema, psoriasis or dry skin. At the time, Elave was being marketed as a unisex product, ("yes, despite its pink packaging!" declares Joanna). Joanna immediately set about re-branding the product, developing it into two separate products: one wash and one cream. However, while Joanna was now Ovelle's Marketing Manager, she essentially had no budget: "a Marketing Manager with no money to do marketing", she recalls. Joanna was beginning to get an insight into the financial side of the business. She was beginning to realise that this long-established family business was in trouble. The company had lost focus; too many products, high overheads and no strategic direction. It was losing money fast, and staff morale was at its lowest. Joanna's father was clearly worried, and with just cause. Joanna began to wonder whether she had made the right decision in joining Ovelle.

The Turnaround

However, just when the business reached crisis point, two private investors were found for Ovelle and things really began to change. For the first time since its establishment, 45 per cent of the Ovelle family business would now be owned by two outsiders. This was clearly an emotional time for the family, especially for Joanna's parents. However, Joanna had a different view. She saw it as a great opportunity to develop and refocus both the company and the entire product range. While the investors – two local businessmen – took a keen interest in the business, they left the day-to-day running of the company to core Ovelle staff. They did, however, attend the company's monthly sales meetings and used their influence with the local banks to leverage a better financial deal for Ovelle. While they had clearly seen potential in the Ovelle product range, it was evident that significant changes would have to be made if the company was to be financially viable and the investors were to get a return on their money. They were going to have to rethink the entire business direction of the company. With Joanna busy working on the company's marketing and promotional strategy, the investors and their external consultants were contemplating a new leader. Joanna was in for a surprise. In May 2000, she was appointed to the role of Managing Director, as she recalls:

> It really came as a shock at the time. In fact, it was a
> shock to everyone. I think, since the obvious choice – my
> brother – was still studying, there was an expectation, par-
> ticularly among the production staff, that an experienced
> outside manager would be brought in to take over. My

father had already indicated that he would step down to focus on product development, so while that part of it was sad, it was sort of expected. It was his proposed replacement that was unexpected.

Realistically, while perhaps not exactly the traditional choice Joanna was the obvious one. She recognised straight away that the business had to change. In fact, she embraced change. She appreciated the true value of the product and could see its potential. She understood the market and was notorious for coming up with new ideas for promoting the product range. If anyone was able to take Ovelle through a period of significant change it was Joanna – and she was going to make lots of changes.

Up until then, the company had no real management team in place. Joanna's parents were both still working in the business as QPs[9] and her father was heavily involved in developing product formulations. Today there are seven staff members on the company's core management team. Furthermore, there had been very little staff training taking place in the business, and one of the first things Joanna did was to introduce appropriate training procedures. Part of her staff training strategy involved generating new ideas from every part of the business through an innovation programme called "Out of the Box" – a highly inclusive initiative which encourages staff to be more creative and encourages team-working.

Communication also featured strongly as a core part of Joanna's new approach, with the primary aim of ensuring that all Ovelle staff were aware of the brand, the brand strategy and the overall direction of the business.

But, when Joanna took over as MD, she also had to make some very tough decisions, decisions that were not always popular. When she joined the business, the company had around eighty staff, including four sales representatives on the road serving the retail market. As part of the new strategic direction of the business, Joanna had to downsize, which inevitably meant redundancies. Joanna moved 50 per cent of the business to wholesalers. Now, Ovelle has a total of fifty staff and no sales representatives on the road. There is just one sales manager with whom Joanna works to negotiate with the big buying groups. Sales are growing and, what's more, they are costing less to manage.

In rationalising her tough decision to take the company's sales reps off the road, Joanna simply explains that it was the most cost effective way of doing business:

> We're good at making product. Why on earth were we trying to break our backs distributing? That's not what we're good at. It was a really tough time, and obviously some jobs had to go and people took that very personally. But the company needed to be taken by the 'scruff of the neck' and some really tough business decisions had to be made. It was really hard for me but, had I not made those sorts of decisions, everyone's life would have been affected because the business would simply not have survived.

Although she had the Elave strategy in her mind long before she realised that the business was in difficulties, there is no doubt that some of the changes Joanna has introduced would simply not have been possible had the business not reached crisis point. In many cases, there was simply no alternative: "that's when a crisis can really help you perform", comments Joanna.

Within a relatively short space of time, Ovelle has significantly refined its product range. In 2000 it had just two products under the Elave range. By 2005 it had fifteen Elave products. It has also developed its export business, which now accounts for around 33 per cent of its turnover. In addition, the company holds a number of long-term agreements to supply UNICEF and the UN, worth in excess of €200,000 annually. Its products and processes had to be audited at length before being awarded the contracts, which it won on an open tender basis. It now also develops and manufactures private label products under contract for Merck Generics UK, Gerard Laboratories and Goldshield Healthcare. In total, including it Elave brand, Ovelle currently manufactures over one hundred products, and its export sales have increased by 121 per cent since 2000.

Given the above, it is not surprising that, in 2004, Joanna was selected as an Ernst & Young Entrepreneur of the Year Award Finalist.[10] Further recognition of her business acumen and innovative thinking came two years later in February 2006, when the Minister for Education and Science appointed Joanna as Chairperson of the Governing Body of Dundalk Institute of Technology (DKIT). Joanna would be DKIT's first female chairperson since the Institute was formally designated as a corporate body in 1992.

Entrepreneurial Traits

Joanna sees herself as a very positive person, an ideas person. She believes that her personal experiences, including being a mother, understanding the value of money and being driven by a desire for financial independence (rather than by money itself) have helped her to become more realistic in life. She can see 'the wood from the trees' and prioritise things in a crisis – important skills to have in the business world. However, when asked what she thinks is the most important entrepreneurial trait, she laughs:

> But I'm not really an entrepreneur you know. An entrepreneur is someone who invents something and then makes money out of it, or at least that's the way I used to think. Now I think it's actually harder to re-energise an existing business rather than start one from scratch.

For Joanna, being a good judge of people is one of the most critical entrepreneurial skills.

> I feel I have recruited really well for the business. Since I took over as MD, I have had the unfortunate experience of having to make people redundant – it's not a nice thing to have to do, believe me. When you run a business, managing people is the biggest draw on your time, and it's important to try and keep your team motivated and happy.

Moving Forward – The Decision to Compete in the Export Market

It has taken Joanna five years to turn Ovelle around from a floundering business to one with the potential to be a real player in the global marketplace. "We have a great team of people here now", says Joanna proudly. "There's a great atmosphere and it's all down to communication. Hey, we don't even have a personnel department".

Ovelle are now gearing up for the expansion phase, which will obviously mean new markets as well as a new export strategy. For example, the scale of the UK market is completely different to Ireland, and securing a major retail chain like Boots could add millions to Ovelle's turnover within the space of a few months. Joanna is planning to double the company's turnover within the next three years, and if she is serious about that then she needs to get really serious about the export business.

With the 'Save your Skin' slogan established alongside the Elave brand, Ovelle will be the first Irish company to market a product range that is completely SLS-free. As Joanna explains:

> I think we are ready now to move from managing a 'dry skin problem' to focusing on the 'worried well'. When it comes to skincare, people are going back to basics, though so-called 'organic' skincare products are still a long way off. There are common chemical additives that can trigger adverse skin reactions, so we have simply removed them from our product range.

There is no doubt that Ovelle's 'Save your Skin' and SLS-free principles have played a critical role in the company's marketing strategy to date. However, the big challenge is how to weave them into the new export strategy to take on the global competitors. From a marketing perspective, the time is right. One-third of children nowadays get eczema – a figure that used to be one in twenty – the increase being largely due to chemicals in washes and harsh perfumes used in soaps. In many ways, concerns about skincare would appear to be developing in the same way as concerns about food; people are starting to check product labels for potentially harmful additives. Concerns over the safety of certain chemicals in skincare products are becoming more common.[11] However, competing at the global level and taking on the big players will inevitably mean more changes within the company – significant further investment, a new recruitment drive and an international marketing campaign. But is Ovelle ready for another major shake-up? Is Joanna? Regardless of what the future holds, it looks as if Joanna is going to be around for a while:

> I really believe in what we are doing now. We are doing something with a lot of integrity; we are the first chemi-cal-safe, skincare range on the market and I am very com-mitted to that. Sometimes, I don't know if I could ever leave this.

NOTES

1   This case was prepared by Dr Colette Henry as the basis for class discussion rather than to illustrate either effective or ineffective handling of a business situation.

2   Colette Henry is Head of Department of Business Studies and Director of the Centre for Entrepreneurship Research, Dundalk Institute of Technology (Colette.henry@ dkit.ie). The author is extremely grateful to Joanna Gardiner for her time and her inspiration in helping to prepare this case.

3   Enterprise Ireland is the State agency responsible for supporting indigenous enter-prises in the manufacturing or internationally traded services sectors.

4   Feed-back.com Ezine, (2004) 'U.S. Consumer Skin Care Products', *Feed-back.com Ezine*, Vol. 7, No. 1 (March), available at: <http://www.feed-back.com/mar04ezine. htm> [accessed 3 April 2006].

5   Research and Markets (2000) 'Toiletries Market Report Plus', *Research and Markets*, available at: <http://www.researchandmarkets.com/reportinfo.asp?report_ id=3906> [accessed 3 April 2006]; Research and Markets (2005) 'Toiletries Market Report Plus', *Research and Markets*, available at: <http://www.researchandmarkets. com/reportinfo.asp?cat_id=0&report_id=307831&q=Toiletries%20Market%20Report %20Plus%20&p=1> [accessed 3 April 2006].

6   As cited in the *New York Times*, 13 July 2003.

7   Deutsch, Claudia H. (2003) 'Scientific Solution to Save Your Skin', *New York Times*, 13 July, as cited by: <http://www.sensualism.com/beauty/skin.html> [accessed 3 April 2006].

8   Epstein, Samuel and Day, Phillip, 'Toxic Chemicals in Toiletries', *Health-Report. co.uk*, available at: <http://www.health-report.co.uk/toxic_toiletries.html> [accessed 3 April 2006].

9   QP (Qualified Person): a recognised term in the pharmaceutical industry for quali-fied and experienced people authorised to test formulations.

10   The Ernst & Young Entrepreneur of the Year Awards recognise the entrepreneurial achievements of Irish businessmen and women. See <http://www.eoy.ie> for further details.

11   See, for example, UK first edition feature, 'How safe are your toiletries', *Express Newspapers*, 14 December 2004.

Exhibit 1
Elave Product Range

elave body wash

250ml   €6.99

elave body oil

250ml   €9.99

elave intensive cream

125ml   €7.99

elave shampoo

250ml   €6.99

elave facial cleanser

250ml   €7.99

elave shower

125ml   €4.49

elave body lotion

250ml   €7.99

elave hand wash

250ml   €6.99

Source: <http://www.elave.ie> (Prices correct at 9 August 2007)

Exhibit 2

Total U.S. Consumer Skin Care Products Market, 1995–2000

(Revenues are in Millions of Dollars at the Retail Level)

Year	Revenues	Growth Rate (%)
1995	2,125.0	–
1996	2,496.0	17.5
1997	2,850.0	14.2
1998	3,270.0	14.7
1999	3,755.0	14.8
2000	4,187.0	11.5

Compound Annual Growth Rate, 1995–2000 = 14.5%
Source: Feedback Research Services
<http://www.feed-back.com/mar04ezine.htm>

Exhibit 3
Article in the *Irish Examiner*

Irish Examiner.com
<http://archives.tcm.ie/irishexaminer/2000/10/21/current/ipage_4.
htm>
21 October 2000

Women should not be fooled by expensive creams
by Linda McGrory

EVERY year Irish women spend millions of pounds on creams and lotions in the hope of finding the secret of eternal youth.

They willingly fork out anything from £10 to £50 for the latest line of anti-wrinkle and cellular renewal potions, the ingredients of which sound more like the dinner menu on the Starship Enterprise.

What they might not realise however, is that the basic formula for many of these expensive creams has been made in Ireland since the 1940s and can be bought for £3 in a chemist.

Silcock's Base, which is made by Ovelle Ltd, Dundalk, is a thick white cream recommended by dermatologists for sensitive and problem skin including conditions such as eczema and psoriasis.

It consists of white petroleum, emulsifying wax and water, the basics of nearly all good moisturisers.

There is no mention of anti oxidants to repair damaged skin cells, alpha hydroxy acids to brighten up the skin or retinol to boost skin cell regrowth.

But it is one of the best basic moisturisers available for skin and is also recommended by leading dermatologists.

Body Shop boss Anita Roddick has rocked the cosmetics world by claiming that most modern cosmetics are 'complete pap'.

Roddick is not so much bothered by the creams' ingredients so much as the makers' claims that they are wonder cures for wrinkles and fine lines, accompanied by advertisements exaggerating the benefits.

Ovelle Ltd agrees that women should not be fooled out of their money by expensive creams and advertising hype.

Unlike multi billion pound cosmetics giants such as Lâncome and Estee Lauder, the company's annual turnover is around £500,000 while its return on Silcock's Base is a modest £100,000 a year.

Marketing manager Joanna Gardiner agrees with Roddick that women are only buying a dream if they think a lotion can reverse the ageing process.

Instead she says women can only hope to look as good as they can for their age by using a good basic moisturiser, sun block and eating a healthy diet. "Silcock's base is basically water and petroleum which is in nearly all moisturising products".

"It might be a bit messy in its generic form but in its refined state such as our Emulave range, and if used with a good sun block and a healthy diet, we believe women can do no better," said Ms Gardiner.

The product is named after a Liverpool dermatologist, Dr Silcock, who used it on Irish patients while on monthly visits to Dublin in the 1930s.

© Irish Examiner, 2000

Peter Fitzgerald Randox[1]

GARVAN WHELAN AND
COLM O'GORMAN[2]

INTRODUCTION

As Peter Fitzgerald waits for his plane to take off from Belfast International Airport, he looks out on to the waters of Lough Neagh. As a youngster, he had played on the shores of this lake and had dreamt of being an explorer who made discoveries and brought them back to his home in Ireland. Now he is managing director of a company that is bringing medical discoveries – made in a laboratory located just a few miles from the lake – to a worldwide market.

His lab is actually a converted hen house and stable, located on his parents' smallholding in rural Co. Antrim. From these humble beginnings, and a rather unpromising economic environment, emerged Randox Laboratories, a producer of medical diagnostic products. In 2005 this privately owned firm had annual revenues of STG£48 million (€70m), with 450 employees in Ireland and another 120 worldwide. Peter Fitzgerald currently owns 98 per cent of the firm and, in 2004, he was named Ernst & Young Entrepreneur of the Year.

As the view of Lough Neagh gets smaller, Peter reflects on his achievements, and on how it all started. He knows that, in order to grow his company, he will have to compete with major players such as Roche, Abbott and Bayer. As he considers potential strategies, he wonders how it will be possible to seriously compete at the global level from his current base in Ireland.

BACKGROUND

Peter Fitzgerald came from a modest background. He was brought up in rural Co. Antrim, near a village called Crumlin, in Northern Ireland. His father worked in a local factory, but his parents also had a smallholding of two acres. This property, on which they kept pigs and hens, brought in extra cash for Peter Fitzgerald's parents, which was used to support Peter's and his older brother's schooling, as his parents were keen on education. His family didn't have a tradition of entrepreneurial activity as such, though in his father's family there would have been small shopkeepers.

> I grew up on a smallholding, in the middle of nowhere. We had a very nice upbringing but it was not privileged; we didn't have a lot of money. My background was not overly religious, but the emphasis was on trying to improve things in life rather than on material possessions.

Reflecting back on his schooling and childhood he described himself as a "slow developer, but I always felt that I could do something". At the local grammar school, Peter had various periods of success and failure: "I went through stages when I was a very mediocre student, and I was quite a slow reader". His parents had to get extra tuition to get him focused back on to his studies. But at around sixteen years of age he started working harder, "very hard", and he managed to get the O Levels, and then moved on to study for A Levels in order to get into university. Towards the end of his secondary education he won some prizes for maths and science subjects. Outside of school he had an active childhood. He spent a lot of time playing sports and participated in other activities, including mountain climbing and athletics. He was a member of the scouts, which involved working with people in groups and teams.

The young Fitzgerald had an interest in science and medicine and, even as a schoolboy, it was always in the back of his mind to make medical discoveries. He had no interest in becoming a medical practitioner; he felt that studying medicine would not allow him to do the research he wanted to do. Reading stories of "Victorian heroes" stimulated his interest in medical research and discoveries:

> I always admired people who would change things, whether it was through exploring or science or medicine.

I liked reading adventure stories, how people overcame adversity. Since I wanted to do medical research, I made up my mind to study biochemistry.

In 1969, Fitzgerald went to the University of Strathclyde, Glasgow, Scotland. His choice of college reflected his desire to live away from home and the fact that the university had a highly regarded biochemistry department. He described the experience of living in Glasgow:

It was actually a very sectarian city and I was quite shocked. It was also very divided, which came out of the gang warfare era. Ironically enough, coming from Northern Ireland, this was the first time I came across such division.

At first, Peter found it difficult to adjust to his new surroundings, but after a while he settled. He describes Strathclyde as "a good working-class university where people had to work very, very hard and no nonsense".

Having graduated from Strathclyde, he completed a Ph.D. in London, in the Masters' Institute of Medical Research, which is the main centre for clinical research in the UK. His area of study was investigating bacterial defence mechanisms. The Institute provided an environment where researchers "were obsessed with medical research and trying to make advances". Three years later, aged twenty-six, he returned to Northern Ireland and went to work at Queen's University as a researcher, rather than moving to the United States to advance his research career. He was well qualified, but was still considered a "novice" in the field and as such he started on a low salary. While working in Queen's University he worked in areas of medical research that were new to him. Commenting on why he returned to Northern Ireland he reflected:

It was a combination of factors. I guess mainly I wanted my own firm so that I would have more control over my own destiny. I have to admit even when I was a teenager I always wanted to create something. I don't know why, but I just felt that I never would fit into a large organisation. I wasn't saying I was an arrogant person – I didn't feel I would be able to play political games very well.

Instead, I wanted to start my own business in medical research from my home environment.

Reflecting on his motives, Fitzgerald described the primary reasons for starting a business: first, an interest in medical research to help find cures; and second the desire to create wealth and employment in south Antrim and throughout Northern Ireland. For Fitzgerald it wasn't a materialistic thing: "you don't have to make a large personal gain, though you do need to make sure that the business is profitable; I think it's important to try and make a difference."

THE OPPORTUNITY

Peter Fitzgerald was looking for ways to start a business for quite a long time. He investigated several possibilities over a number of years. Eventually he came across an area of the market called medical diagnostics, which was dominated by large German and American multinational companies (see Exhibit 1).

Medical diagnostics was – and still is – a growing market, because of the need to identify the nature of a patient's illness through diagnostic tests as accurately and as quickly as possible. Peter's awareness of the importance of this sector came about because, in his spare time, he "went cold-calling around hospitals". His idea was the result of:

> Talking to all sorts of companies and just generally my own thinking. I never had any contacts as such. I would just go into a hospital and ask to speak with someone with responsibility for medical research and new product development.

Peter would ask these individuals about the problems and issues they faced and discussed how medical research could help. From these discussions, he concluded that medical diagnostics was an area that had potential. He admits that he "didn't know anything about the industry" but he was enthusiastic and he decided to start working on his idea. Peter was aged twenty-eight at that time. Friends and family contributed bits and pieces; he got some old parts of equipment thrown out of the university and he used local builders "to fix things up". His laboratory needed a home, so he "converted the hen house and stable into a lab". The business was started on a part-time basis and he developed products in the evenings and weekends and had them evaluated in the local hospitals to see if they worked. The initial results were encouraging. Then he arrived at a decision point. In order to meet customer requirements, it came to the stage where he had to buy "a freeze dryer" – an expensive piece of production equipment.

At the time, Peter was saving money in order to buy a house. He was "at a crossroads". It wasn't feasible to continue on a minor scale by carrying out tests in small batches. He knew it was "a big step", but he decided to make some personal sacrifices and put the money from his own savings into the business. In addition, he convinced his father that his ideas were worthwhile.

> There was no great wealth behind me. My father had inherited a few more acres of land from his father; so a bit of money from the family went into it, not a lot, just a wee bit. That allowed us to buy the freeze-drying equipment and since the business was continuing to develop, I left my full-time job.

LEAVING FULL-TIME EMPLOYMENT

Fitzgerald had, at this stage, what could be described as a relatively safe career path in front of him. His colleagues, friends and family reacted with surprise when they heard of his decision to leave full-time employment and start a business:

> People did think I was daft. Certainly staff in the university thought I was crazy to be doing this. My friends and relations all said that it was a strange thing to do – to give up a safe, secure job.

When he told people that he was starting a company manufacturing diagnostics, their initial response was not encouraging. They pointed out that such a project "could not be done" and that "it would never work out". However, Peter Fitzgerald was never particularly concerned about the risk of failure, and he never contemplated giving up:

> I was never really worried about risk. In one sense I had nothing to lose because I had nothing. That is more or less

it; I remember I had a sheepskin coat, and that was about all I had.

The Emerging Firm

During the period 1981–1982 Fitzgerald worked on developing the products on his own. He described this time as "a very hard, difficult and tough period". He had no income from sales revenue, so he lived off his limited savings: "I had nothing; I just spent the time working". At this stage he felt he was making little progress. His family organised an overseas holiday for him: "I came back from the holiday, completely refreshed and revitalised, and a lot of things fell into place". The firm was incorporated as Randox Laboratories in 1982, when Peter Fitzgerald was thirty-two years old.

It was a tough time to start a business in Northern Ireland, as 1982 was one of the worst years of the "Troubles", with bombings and shootings taking place almost every week, and a political process that was in stalemate. His next task was to find customers. He received very little support from organisations in Northern Ireland in the early stages. Peter later reflected that, "often a prophet in his own land is never accepted". In England, it was difficult to convince hospitals that a small company in the outback of Co. Antrim could manufacture and deliver quality clinical diagnostic products. The hospitals in the other parts of Ireland and those in Scotland and Wales were more supportive. Eventually, the orders started to come in as customers came to realise that his products were technically superior to those of his larger competitors and could be delivered faster. Peter recalls that, thanks to a combination of "persistence and charm", the company "slowly but relentlessly" built up a customer base and started to develop overseas markets as well.

During the period up to 1985, the business experienced growth in sales, new products and employees. However, in financial terms, "they were struggling". For a period of about nine months it couldn't pay its suppliers. This was a serious situation for the firm. Without continuing supplies of medical equipment and packaging materials, it couldn't meet the growing number of customer orders. Exhibit 2 shows extracts from the company's balance sheet for 1984 and for other years (see Exhibit 2).

Peter Fitzgerald knew that the business might close down, but he wouldn't accept it. His response was to go out and sell more products. He also decided to go and meet with his suppliers and creditors personally.

> I was honest with them, and said, "I have no money, can't pay you, don't know when I can pay you, but hopefully I can in a few months."

These meetings included visits to the bank, where he had an overdraft that was significantly over its agreed limit. His problems were compounded by the fact that he ran out of room in the converted stable and hen house and he needed more space. During this time, Fitzgerald recalled that he had "setbacks and failures all the time". But his attitude was that, "it depends what you call failure". He commented that "if something didn't work", he didn't really regard it as "failing". Instead, he viewed it as "just another stage in getting the right result". He gradually traded his way out of the financial crisis by increasing sales and ensuring that the money was collected promptly.

INVESTING IN R&D

Even with continuing growth in sales, Fitzgerald believed that he had to "ramp up R&D" in order to improve the range of products offered to his customers. In spite of receiving advice to the contrary, he hired two research and development (R&D) staff, and he moved the research facilities to a new premises. Exhibit 3 contains extracts from the company's (and some of its competitors') income statements (see Exhibit 3).

Fitzgerald explained the rationale for putting resources into R&D as follows:

> We couldn't see how we were ever going to get anything at all without developing more products. No point in having a few wee products. We had to make improvements to lengthen the life cycle of our products and we had to keep expanding our range to be interesting to our distributors.

This commitment to R&D required extra finance. He received many refusals when he approached banks and government agencies for funding. So, how did he react?

> I just kept going. I suppose I expected the 'nos'; but I knew I would have to find somebody who would have faith in my ideas and discoveries.

He eventually found such a person: an Ulster Bank manager in Belfast, who lent him STG£30,000 (€44,000), unsecured. The bank continued to finance the company's research and marketing operations on this basis for a number of years. When further investment in R&D was required, the firm was supported by two local banks: Ulster Bank and Bank of Ireland. Peter commented: "it would have been very difficult without the aid of banks supporting me in the early stages".

Fitzgerald considered venture capital as a form of finance many times, especially in the early days. During the mid 1980s he received an offer from a US venture capitalist. Peter recalled that he was visited by an American who "interrogated me thoroughly to see if I was a worthwhile investment". The venture capital company offered STG£1m (€1.45m) for a 40 per cent shareholding in Randox. This was considered to be a very good offer, taking into account that annual turnover was approximately STG£80,000 (€116,000) at the time. However, Fitzgerald felt that he wasn't ready to relinquish a large share of the company to investors who might not agree with his policy of reinvesting profits into R&D.

MANAGING THE GROWTH OF RANDOX LABORATORIES

Since the late 1980s Randox Laboratories has experienced high levels of growth, approximately 60 per cent per annum. Central to this growth has been Fitzgerald's commitment to creativity and experimentation:

> Sometimes I find the best decisions are radical. I tend to ignore the possibility of failure and just play around the edges. I try to make as many radical choices as possible. For instance I will hire younger people to work here, not just to keep salaries low, but to bring in fresh ideas and approaches.

Over the years the two main challenges for Fitzgerald have been, "to keep to the forefront in the development of biochip diagnostic systems through R&D" and, "to develop the brand throughout the world" (see Exhibit 4).

It has been very important for Fitzgerald to make customers aware of the Randox brand and "what the company stands for". Randox now has 150 sales people around the world. In order to achieve this level of growth, Fitzgerald has identified a number of issues that he had to deal with, including:

- Continuing innovative research practices in order to keep ahead of the competition by developing market relevant products.
- Dealing with new customers, distributors and export markets.
- Financing increased levels of activity.
- Hiring and co-ordinating the efforts of staff from technical, financial and other backgrounds.

As the MD of a medium-sized organisation, how does Peter Fitzgerald manage these issues?

Managing R&D as a Competitive Advantage
Fitzgerald attributes his company's competitive edge to its investment in R&D and the knowledge acquired. He believes that you don't have to be a large organisation to have bright ideas. He is aware that Randox is a relatively small company in the worldwide diagnostics market. Exhibit 5 illustrates the size difference in terms of turnover between Randox and three of its main competitors (see Exhibit 5).

The approach in Randox is to develop prize-winning science and to apply the findings to customer needs. Fitzgerald describes his much larger competitors as "dinosaurs" who are not responding quickly enough to changing market conditions. He believes that there is "a competitive edge in using your own brain power" and that this does not require a lot of resources. He believes "smart ideas" come from self-belief:

> I am not saying we are more creative but we have gener-
> ated many new ideas. Our attitude is based on self-belief
> and radical thinking; questioning and challenging the old
> way of doing things. Large well-established organisations

are not necessarily doing things the right way. Trying to discover a better way of doing things is very important. My work here is about learning; we are seeking new approaches and methods.

Fitzgerald believes that collaborations with universities and client laboratories are important to developing his R&D capabilities: "the more clinical trials and commissions and discussions we have with research partners, the better". He cautions, however, about over-relying on university research groups to develop the products. He argues that many researchers in the medical and healthcare sector have not considered the patient when they are trying to develop new products or processes. This is reflected in their entrenched systems and technologies, which prevent researchers (especially those attached to large organisations) from asking how to improve the diagnostic process in order to meet changing customer needs.

Managing Exports and Distribution

Fitzgerald has been very aggressive in exporting, a key requirement for his firm given the relatively small size of the local market. One of the first countries he exported to was the Netherlands, followed by the United States. He then developed markets in parts of Germany and other European countries. His approach in the early days was to attend exhibitions. Fitzgerald's view is that Randox can sell to any country in the world, either through established distribution channels or through direct sales. Interestingly, he suggests the more complex the market, the better it is for his company. He claims that this is so because Randox now understands and appreciates the most appropriate procedures for dealing with a wide range of cultural and regulatory issues relevant to each new market.

Distributors have been central to Randox's growth. Managing the selection, retention and replacement of distributors is a "never-ending process". Fitzgerald's view of distributors is that:

> Like everything, some are very good at some stages, some go bad after a while, so they vary immensely in their abilities but they are a very cost-effective way to get to the market if you get the right ones. You have to constantly look at the quality of work coming through.

Financing Growth

Growth in Randox has been financed mainly by reinvesting profits. Exhibit 2 contains extracts from the company's balance sheets. Other sources include bank loans, creditors and government grants. Fitzgerald is quite positive about the support he received from the banks. He argues that, in dealing with bankers, the challenge for the entrepreneur is to:

> Convince them that you are dedicated and reasonably sensible about the money you withdraw for personal reasons. If you keep the lines of communication open, you should get good support from the banks.

While Fitzgerald has received offers to sell either part, or all, of Randox, his view is that, as a private company, he has been able to take a long-term view in developing the firm. He believes his competitors, much larger organisations, have not done this. He suggests that because of shareholder concerns, management in larger firms have not had the vision or the courage to look beyond short-term profits.

FITZGERALD AS A MANAGER

Reflecting on his role in the company, Fitzgerald claims that time is the most valuable resource for any manager. In the early stages of the development of Randox he found that he had to be involved in all aspects of the business, including research, sales, operations and finance. But he quickly realised he needed structures with roles and responsibilities assigned. For example, he appointed an R&D manager, a manager with responsibility for the brand name and accounts management, a manager of manufacturing and operations, and a person in charge of administration.

He described his function as "master of many crafts, a jack-of-all-trades", a role he still plays. On his ability to delegate, he reflected:

> I don't think I'm a control freak, I think that is the real danger in starting a business; I wouldn't like to think I was. I do think there are certain things that have to be controlled. Somebody has to be in charge. All I know is that there have been times when I don't get involved, and things don't go as well as you think they should. But sometimes you have to let people learn by their own mistakes.

79

As an example of his approach to management, he outlined how he works closely with his internal and external accountants. Every morning, his first meeting is with his financial advisors, to review recent and planned expenditure. He discovered at an early stage of his career that financial information is the basis for making important decisions. Since the early days of the firm's trading history, Peter has used accountants to compile the necessary figures, and he always consults with his financial advisors to get their opinion. However, he has always believed that it is very important for people to realise that he has an understanding of the accounting figures and terminology.

His attitude to financial figures is further illustrated in his description of a recent staff encounter:

> I was coming back on the plane from London the other day with a colleague who was a research scientist. I spent a fair bit of time showing her the elements of financial reports – various aspects, such as gross margin, budgets, cash flows, etc. I feel it's very important for all managers to understand where money is being spent and where it comes from.

Randox Today

The company continues to invest in R&D, and has registered over forty patents for new products and processes. It has over 30,000 clients, mostly hospital laboratories, in 130 countries. Recently, the firm has launched a new diagnostic system utilising protein biochip technology. Randox has spent STG£75m (€109m) developing this product. Over 190 scientists from around the world (including the Nobel Prize-awarding Karilinska Institute in Sweden and St James' Hospital in Dublin) were involved in the project. The product has a wide range of therapeutic applications and according to Fitzgerald:

> Our diagnostic system has the potential to revolutionise healthcare worldwide by providing greater information from patient samples than is currently possible. It will also enable clinicians to use DNA and molecular technology to pinpoint potentially life-threatening conditions earlier.

Fitzgerald believes that Randox now has a platform technology that will dramatically increase the firm's pipeline of products coming through, allowing it to leapfrog current technology and achieve further significant growth.

Peter Fitzgerald's success has been recognised by a series of awards – his company is four times winner of the Queen's Award for Export Achievement. In 2003, on behalf of Randox, Peter accepted the MacRobert Award, which is the UK's most prestigious engineering award (other finalists for the prize included Rolls Royce plc).

FUTURE CHALLENGES

As the plane descended, Peter could see the rough seas near the runway of JFK International Airport in New York. His thoughts shifted from the past to the present, and to the challenges that lie ahead for both himself and Randox. The company is still relatively small in comparison to the large multinational firms that dominate the industry. His recent market research indicates that Randox presently supplies only 2.2 per cent of all tests conducted in the worldwide clinical diagnostic sector. This means that there is substantial room for market development in the future. However, Peter's continued success means that multinational competitors will react to Randox's assault on their dominant market position, with firms such as Roche, Abbott or Bayer seeing him as a potential takeover target. Reflecting back on how Randox has developed to date, Peter wonders if he can now transform his company into one of the leading medical diagnostic suppliers in the world. The key challenge now for Peter is how to develop a global organisation from his base in Ireland.

NOTES

1   This case was prepared by Garvan Whelan and Dr Colm O'Gorman as the basis for class discussion rather than to illustrate either effective or ineffective handling of a business situation.

2   Garvan Whelan lectures at the Institute of Technology Tallaght, Dublin (garvan.whelan@ittdublin.ie) and Colm O'Gorman lectures at University College Dublin (colm.ogorman@ucd.ie). The authors are extremely grateful to Peter Fitzgerald for his time and his inspiration in helping to prepare this case.

Exhibit 1
The Medical Diagnostics Market

Diagnostics can help healthcare systems use precious resources more efficiently and can create economic value. Although diagnostic tests provide the basis for about two-thirds of all medical decisions, they account for only 1 per cent of healthcare expenditure. For many years, new technologies were regarded as cost drivers. But looking at the treatment process as a whole, it is clear that innovative diagnostics can help make healthcare delivery more cost-effective while also providing a sounder basis for medical decision-making. And they can help physicians tailor treatment more closely to the individual needs of their patients. Modern tests, for example, can make it easier to determine the best medicine and dosage for a particular patient. As a result, patients receive better treatment and are less apt to suffer serious, costly adverse events.

Source: Roche AG 2004, Annual Report

Exhibit 2
Extracts from Balance Sheets of Randox and Competitors

	Randox 1984	Randox 1999	Randox 2004
	€000s	€000s	€000s
Current Assets	87	19,426	34,841
Current Liabilities	207	7,884	14,552
Long Term Loans	51	3,860	27,070
Ordinary Share Capital	22	131	131
Preference Shares	—	87	5,800
Retained Profits	(17)	17,752	10,354
Shareholders' Funds	5	17,970	16,285
	Abbot 2004	**Bayer 2004**	**Roche 2004**
	€000s	€000s	€000s
Current Assets	8,496,012	20,729,000	2,751,726
Current Liabilities	5,402,306	8,963,000	17,310
Long Term Loans	3,789,516	7,228,000	554,577
Ordinary Share Capital	2,349,572	1,870,000	102,581
Preference Shares	–	–	–
Retained Profits	8,988,884	8,962	5,510,504
Shareholders' Funds	11,338,456	1,878,962	5,613,085

Source: Approximations based on companies' Annual Reports

Exhibit 3

Extracts from Income Statements of Randox and Competitors

	Randox 1984	Randox 1989	Randox 1994	Randox 1999
	€000s	€000s	€000s	€000s
Turnover – Diagnostics	117	1,338	9,242	22,014
R&D – Diagnostics	46	229	2,797	6,142
	Randox 2004	Abbot 2004	Bayer 2004	Roche 2004
	€000s	€000s	€000s	€000s
Turnover – Diagnostics	46,873	2,673,592	1,322,000	3,244,299
R&D – Diagnostics	13,337	230,515	91,218	293,639

Source: Approximations based on companies' Annual Reports

Exhibit 4
Biochips and Diagnostics

The size of the worldwide diagnostics market was approximately $26 billion (€20.6 billion) in 2004. There are two types of diagnostic tests: *in vivo* and *in vitro*. *In vivo* diagnostics involve direct examination of the body using X-rays, electrocardiograms (ECG), etc. *In vitro* diagnostics involve analysis of samples of cells, blood and other fluids taken from the body.

Randox has developed biochip-based products and services for the *in vitro* diagnostics market. This global market was worth approximately $18 billion (€14 billion) in 2004. The biochip, also called a microarray or lab on a chip, combines electronics and biology for research and diagnosis. These devices can store and carry out multiple analyses on very small amounts of biological material.

Sources: Sysmex Annual Report 2005, LeadDiscovery Consulting 2005, *Electronic Business*, May 2005.

Exhibit 5
**Comparison of Randox to Competitors in Terms
of Turnover for 2004 – Diagnostics**

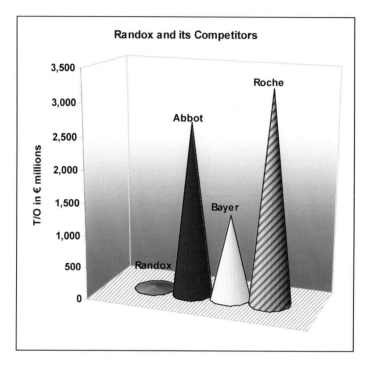

Jerry Kennelly
Stockbyte[1]

BREDA O'DWYER AND ANN SEARS[2]

INTRODUCTION

It's nine in the morning and Jerry Kennelly, CEO and founder of
Stockbyte, has just finished another international conference call. His
technical team are working on location preparing the next edition of royalty-free images for sale to newspapers, magazines and advertising companies around the world. Stockbyte operates in a highly competitive
global marketplace, where innovation and advanced search technologies
offer the competitive edge. Established by Jerry in 1997, the company is
driven by creativity, quality and a strong desire to be first. Stockbyte is a
serious contender in the industry, competing against major players like
Getty Images, Photodisc and Bill Gates' Corbis.

A red light on Jerry's desk indicates another incoming call. Jerry takes
it, but there's a crisis. There's been a mudslide at one of the Asian photo-
shooting locations and it is feared that the models, photographers, stylists
and make-up artists are all trapped. Action needs to be taken. Someone
needs to be creative and think fast. Jerry springs into action!

INDUSTRY STRUCTURE

Stockbyte is operating within the royalty-free stock photography sector, a
highly competitive and aggressive global industry. According to Patrick
Donehue, Vice President of Photographer Relations at Corbis, the global
market is estimated to be worth $2 billion; 75 per cent (approximately
$1.5 billion) is in the corporate sector. Stockbyte is a serious contender
within the industry and, in 2003, was ranked third in the world by Font

Shop, Germany's largest distributor of royalty-free imagery. There are a number of competitors operating within this industry, the larger of which include Getty Images, Photodisc and Corbis (which is owned by Bill Gates). However, there are also many smaller competitors operating in the marketplace (see <http://www.fotosearch.com> for a listing of royalty-free photo publishers). One such smaller competitor is called iStockphoto, which has decided to grow via a partnership with Getty Images. Other smaller companies have already been purchased by Getty Images and Corbis. It would appear that the two largest competitors are on the acquisition trail.

Although Corbis has been in the marketplace for sometime, 2004 was the first time that the company was cash flow positive. It also grew through acquisition in 2004 by purchasing the German competitor Zefa for $211 million. In comparison to Corbis, Stockbyte has been profitable since the founding of the business. Stockbyte is currently in a partnership deal with Getty Images, who have approximately 30 per cent of the market. In 2005 Getty Images purchased Amana and Digital Vision for over $200 million. Jonathan Klein, co-founder and CEO of Getty Images, expanded on its growth strategies by stating, "it will be driven by the areas where we wish to expand – international, editorial, related services like assignment and asset management; it could also be international agents and image partners".

STOCKBYTE – THE COMPANY

Stockbyte was established in 1997 after Jerry Kennelly noticed a gap in the marketplace. He understood that he had something to offer, as there was a requirement for high quality imagery, and he knew that he could satisfy the market. Jerry's core competency within the marketplace was his knowledge of the product. His background was in photography and he grew up in a family business – the weekly regional *Kerry's Eye* newspaper. In 1981 he started his first business, Newsfax – a transmission service for news pictures – and this grew to the publishing of corporate newsletters in all thirty-two counties of the island of Ireland. He became exposed to CD Publishing – burning material onto a CD – in the early 1990s and he knew that this was the future that he wanted to explore as a business venture.

When Stockbyte started it needed additional funding and the company opted to source funding from venture capitalists (VCs). It successfully received VC funding and Stockbyte soon became the first company in Kerry to buy out its VC investment. As Jerry said, "VCs usually get rid of you", which was not something that Jerry wanted for his company. He wanted to remain in control. Stockbyte needed the financial injection in the initial start-up stages. ACT Venture Capital bought a 25 per cent stake in the company and then purchased an additional 5 per cent in 2000. However, by late 2003, Stockbyte was in a position to completely buy out the VC company for an undisclosed sum, as Jerry explains:

> We had a frank discussion in 2003, where I told them that if they wanted to stay in, they had to put in more money without getting any more equity. They accepted the logic of the argument, and we bought them out.

Jerry knows that his business depends on Stockbyte's ability to easily manage, license and distribute high quality digital images to its customers. Thus, Stockbyte prides itself on being the best website for filtering images, making it easy for customers to find what they need amongst the company's themed collection of images. Stockbyte's website can filter for price, people, gender, age, ethnicity, copy space, cut out, colour, orientation and indoor/outdoor; it can also subfilter within those categories. Indeed, according to Jerry:

> No-one filters like Stockbyte. Get as tough as you want with our search engine. Avoid the stuff you don't need. Click the things you do. Refine or broaden. You'll end up with a good, solid image selection – ranked by relevance and delivered so fast you might even get home on time (see <http://www.stockbyte.com/advanced_search_info.php>).

As Jerry further explains, "a sub on a newsdesk or an advertising executive can source an image on our website in a matter of seconds" (see Exhibit 1).

But what exactly has made Stockbyte successful? Is it Jerry's entrepreneurial personality, or is it the business idea that he created to fill a gap in the marketplace? Some may argue that the company would have been successful regardless of who had spotted the opportunity and filled the gap. While others would accept that it is Jerry's drive and vision that has made Stockbyte the success it is today.

Currently, Stockbyte employs over forty people in its Tralee head-quarters, with additional facilities in London, England and Wilmington, Ohio, USA. Jerry and his wife Johanna are the sole shareholders of Stockbyte.

In 2005, Jerry won the Ernst & Young Entrepreneur of the Year Award in the Emerging Technologies category. This is only one of the awards that the organisation has won over the years. However, this particular award has given the organisation more publicity than the other awards combined to date.

COMPANY PRODUCTS

Stockbyte offers a royalty-free stock photography library of over 85,000 high quality royalty-free images. It creates generic images for newspapers, magazines, advertising companies and large commercial organisations. During 2006, Stockbyte plans to produce 4,000 images per month to add to its collection.

A Stockbyte image is essentially "a combination of talents – stylists and photographers advised by art directors who are aware of contemporary trends and the requirements of modern stock photography users". This image is a combination of both a product and a service. Stockbyte needs to understand that the added value for the customer is contributed by both the product and the service.

According to Jerry:

> When you are into photography, it is like having a sense of art or music. You're looking at a shot, figuring out how you are going to take it, crafting it in your mind. It's a visual literacy.

This is one of Jerry's core competencies. But the "Stockbyte product" is about much more than this. It is about the creative ability and competency to "research and know" the customer's mind, even before they do. It is about providing any visitor to the website with the ability to "creatively search images, provide creative light boxes for potential use and download images of up to 100MB in minutes". The Stockbyte product is about saving its customers, like Saatchi & Saatchi, valuable and expensive business time. The value of this time-saving may be due to Stockbyte's ability to use advanced search technology. Stockbyte pioneered the use of search filtration, which "allows creatives to quickly filter out images they don't need from search results – using criteria like age, race, location and gender to save creatives valuable time". This would seem to imply that the company's core competency is the ability of the company to integrate all of these factors into a "timely globally relevant new image".

Stockbyte's "product portfolio" includes the following categories:

➢ Abstract and background images	➢ Nature images
➢ Animal images	➢ Object images
➢ Arts and entertainment images	➢ People images
➢ Business images	➢ Science and medicine images
➢ Celebration and holiday images	➢ Society and culture images
➢ Drink images	➢ Sports and recreation images
➢ Education images	➢ Health and beauty images
➢ Food images	➢ Industry and transportation images
➢ Lifestyle images	➢ Technology and communication images

The above portfolio reinforces Jerry Kennelly's belief that, at Stockbyte, "we are the ready-to-wear suits of the image business, offering convenience, style and something different".

The success of this portfolio requires effective and efficient management, continuous awareness and reviews of the needs of the marketplace. Companies in this industry need to continually conduct market research to anticipate trends. Stockbyte prides itself in using information effectively. It is critical for stock photography companies to keep abreast of fashion trends, international magazines, a variety of TV shows and media in general. This is the source of new product ideas and anticipation of future needs of the marketplace. It is equally important to "purge" any old products from the portfolio.

The need to be constantly up to date with required images has obvious consequences for the development of new products. This in turn has implications for the new product development process in a company like Stockbyte. Essentially the stock photography is led by the advertising industry, which in turn is required to stay at the cutting edge of contemporary styles. Ultimately this requires a contemporary approach to product development using cross-function, creative new product venture teams. The cutting edge of this industry also dictates the need for short product life cycles. Jerry Kennelly is used to working to deadlines and thrives in this type of industry. He is quoted as saying, "I can't afford to waste time, it's a dogfight out there and we are one of the most significant players in the business. We need to keep our edge and we do so by providing the type of images which the media and other companies want to buy."

PRODUCTION PROCESS

The planning stage of Stockbyte's operation takes place in Tralee, Co. Kerry. This typically takes about two months. The shooting stage takes place on location around the world, and this takes another two months. The post-production stage takes the material around the world for a final two months. During the post-production stage the material is sent to England for editing, then on to Hong Kong for scanning and retouching, and then back to Tralee for final quality control. Thus, the whole process from conception to commercialisation takes about six months.

Stockbyte operates under the principle of high standards of quality, which it believes to be fundamental to its success in the business, as Jerry explains:

> Our success is down to our standards and the fact that our pictures are better than our rivals'. We refuse to compromise on our pictures. If that means renting a 747 aircraft for one picture, we will rent it, simple as that.

Jerry's refusal to compromise, however, did not stop him from growing his business by going after a lower end of the market. He knew that would require a separate brand and so launched Stockdisc, which focuses on creating aggressively priced, carefully researched stock photography on CD and online (see <http://www.stockdisc.com>). As Stockdisc grows, it may require its own Strategic Business Unit and relevant strategic support (see Exhibit 2).

CUSTOMERS

Currently, Stockbyte has over two million customers worldwide. The customers are made up of business-to-business (B2B) customers and business-to-consumer (B2C) customers. They range from large multinational companies such as AOL, Weight Watchers, Gillette, Avon, Walt Disney, Macmillan Publishing, Coca Cola, Time Magazine, Saatchi & Saatchi and the BBC, to individual private consumers. The images are used for newspapers, advertising campaigns, company brochures and magazine illustrations.

Customers are reached by using a combination of direct and indirect channels of distribution, spanning 120 distributors in over seventy different countries. Customers buy from a catalogue of images – either individual images or a group of images for a specific price. The catalogue of images is available online for the customer to view. The transaction can be done totally by e-commerce, with the customer able to pay and download the images instantaneously. Alternatively, the customer can receive the images on CD. Upon purchase, the customer is free to use the images in any way they wish (up to ten licences with each image). However, they are prohibited from using the images for pornography and defamatory, libellous or otherwise unlawful use. Stockbyte operates a three-tier pricing policy. These are described as Platinum, Gold and Silver image pricing (see <http://www.stock byte.com>).

Developing customer relationships is important to Stockbyte. The company has a call centre located in Tralee, which supports customer queries and helps build customer relations. It advertises its toll-free numbers on its brochures and websites so customers know how they can get in direct contact with staff of the organisation. Maintaining and building customer relations is fundamental to the future success of Stockbyte and Stockdisc. Technological developments in the area of customer relationship management (CRM) provide Stockbyte with the tools for effective account management for both brands. Stockbyte uses direct mail campaigns in Europe and North America, and staff also attend various trade shows to target its customers. It goes without saying that a company such as Stockbyte relies heavily on its e-commerce website as an effective promotional tool (see <http://www. stockbyte.com>).

Dealing with Change

Stockbyte's culture is to be flexible, innovative and adaptable. The company has been learning since it began. The first major problem that the company had to deal with was the brand name in France. Stockbyte was sued in the French High Court over its original brand name; it gave up the name in France and developed the name "Stockbyte". From then on, the company had to be flexible, adaptable and willing to change when necessary.

During the embryonic stages of the company Jerry took many of the photographs himself. However, over time, Jerry's skills were required in other areas of the business. Stockbyte was required to outsource photographers, make-up artists and stylists when on location. This can amount to as many as fifty people being employed at a single location. The company has very good procedures and systems operating abroad which allows it to work efficiently and to tight deadlines.

Customer buying behaviour is constantly monitored by the company, with sales data analysed by data mining. Trends are noticed and worked on by the creative team to develop concepts. Information is the key for Stockbyte, with each transaction representing information for the company, as Jerry comments:

> I have modelled my business on Bill Gates' sterling work –
> *Business @ the Speed of Thought*. Gates' understanding
> of leveraging the information that exists in your business
> to its maximum drives many of the initiatives that have
> secured our position in our industry today. We are constantly learning from our customers, it is our customers
> who tell us what works and, most importantly, what doesn't work. For example, there's a greater demand for
> images with mixed-race families in the USA and in
> Europe. We are conscientious about new product development and about listening to our customers. In the post-
> September 11 and post-dot.com era there's been a greater
> move towards simplicity and towards more real images.

It is clear that Stockbyte listens closely to changes in the marketplace and adapts accordingly.

JERRY – THE ENTREPRENEUR – BEING FIRST

There is no doubt that Jerry likes being first. As noted above, Stockbyte was the first company in Kerry to seek and receive venture capital funding in 1997. Stockbyte was also the first significant European publisher of royalty-free stock photography. In 1999, Stockbyte was the first company on the island of Ireland to offer down-loadable e-commerce by way of virtual CDs. It was instant gratification for both the customers and the company. In 2002, Stockbyte was included in the Deloitte Technology Irish Fast 50. In 2003, it won the DHL Exporter of the Year Award. Stockbyte is also the first company in Kerry to win the Ernst & Young Entrepreneur of the Year Award in the category of Emerging Technologies. "Stockbyte pioneered industry standards for verification of model releases, and are the only stock photo company in the world to offer 24/7 downloads of model releases or such third party verification of its legal safety standards."

Jerry's definition of an entrepreneur is "value creation". But it may also be about the gut instinct and self-belief. While working the Apple Mac computers in the early 1990s, Jerry Kennelly identified a niche in the market and set up a pre-press company in Tralee to provide colour scanning, film and proof services for publishers and design teams. He knew it had a limited lifespan, despite it being profitable. Jerry realised that technology was beginning to move at a fast pace and that digital imaging would quickly replace his business. He knew there was a market for high-quality generic pictures. He knew that most of the publishers could not afford the copyright-protected images. Jerry created ten different CD titles to showcase his pictures. Above all else, Jerry Kennelly had lived and slept photography. He had taken pictures professionally since his teens as part of his family business. "It was a no-brainer to me that this was going to be a great business", he said. Once he showcased his ten CDs he flew to San Francisco to launch his business and came home with his first sales and distribution network. "I was working from the gut; the whole thing was about belief", says Jerry.

But success was not just about the "gut". It was also about hard work, attention to deadlines and spotting and responding to evolving opportunities. The teamwork within the organisation deserves recognition, as Jerry explains: "our team have been disciplined and clear in our focus for excellence".

ENTREPRENEURIAL SPIRIT WITHIN THE ORGANISATION

Stockbyte's mission in life includes a few simple rules:

1. Exceed expectations.
2. Be ourselves – passionately creative.
3. Craft the most relevant images to the highest standard.
4. Leverage the best technology online and off.
5. Enjoy the ride.

Jerry says that the family business created by his parents helped him establish Stockbyte: "a person can get the bug, some people are hungry, some people are not". Jerry himself is hungry and he wants to nurture the intrapreneurial spirit within his organisation. He grew up in a family business where his father, Padraig Kennelly, was:

> The quality-obsessed creative genius and my mother Joan was the financial wizard who always kept the ship afloat, despite how desperate the financial situation was in his early years. That experience from early childhood has always given me a clear understanding of the art of the possible (see Exhibit 3).

Jerry instils a high work ethic within the organisation. "We are quality-focused and we strive to be the best we can be. If that means working 24 hours straight, so be it", says Jerry. His response to ranking third in the world for royalty-free stock photography is simply, "it is proof that clever, creative people can take on the giants and win, from Kerry."

FUTURE GROWTH CHALLENGES

Stockbyte/Stockdisc is now the largest privately held, royalty-free stock photography company by sales, experiencing 50 per cent year-on-year profit growth. The company has chosen not to license images from other companies. All creative production costs have been financed upfront by Stockbyte. Both brands (Stockbyte and Stockdisc) are now in the unique position of wholly owning all of their imagery, providing profitability and flexibility as new business models evolve.

So Where Next?

The company may stick to what works and continue to grow privately or it may plan a route of strategic alliances. If the company chooses to go it alone it will need to decide which growth strategy to follow. The growth of any organisation is possible through two major routes – market and/or product development. Footage for the movie industry would appear to present a new market opportunity. However, expanding the product portfolio to include Asian models and images creates product development opportunities for the company. With Getty Images buying up more market share and becoming partners with a number of smaller competitors, including Stockbyte itself, what is the future for the company? Should Stockbyte respond to the rumours and sell out to Getty? Would this be a good move? As Jerry puts it:

> I suppose it would come as no big surprise if we sold out, but I want to keep the business while I am still adding sustainable value to it. We are looking at other opportunities to leverage our intellectual property portfolio. The company is unique in that we own the rights to all of our images. However, the subscription model cannot be ignored. The imagery that's available in this sector today falls far behind the standards expected by creative users, but the model is an attractive one. We've got some great ideas on how we can create a wonderful value proposition and increase the group's market share in the global imagery marketplace.

Stockbyte needs to consider how to grow and develop within this aggressive, global, competitive marketplace. The creative powers that Jerry learned as part of his family business and from his role model – his father – may well help Jerry in his future decisions and application of the optimum strategy for his company.

But, before Jerry can ponder over the strategic direction of this award-winning company, he needs to deal with the crisis in Asia. He heads to the airport planning to travel to the destination of the mudslide to assess the crisis. As he is boarding the plane, he receives a text message from the press concerning the possible closure of the much-rumoured Getty buyout.

As Jerry reads the text a broad smile appears on his face. What's next for Jerry?

NOTES

1   This case was prepared by Breda O'Dwyer and Ann Sears as the basis for class discussion rather than to illustrate either effective or ineffective handling of a business situation.

2   Breda O'Dwyer and Ann Sears lecture at the Institute of Technology, Tralee (breda.odwyer@staff.ittralee.ie; ann.sears@staff.ittralee.ie). The authors are extremely grateful to Jerry Kennelly for his time and his inspiration in helping to prepare this case.

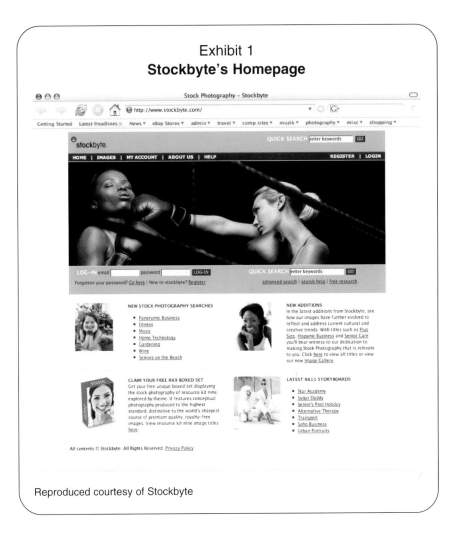

Exhibit 1
Stockbyte's Homepage

Reproduced courtesy of Stockbyte

Exhibit 2
Stockdisc's Homepage

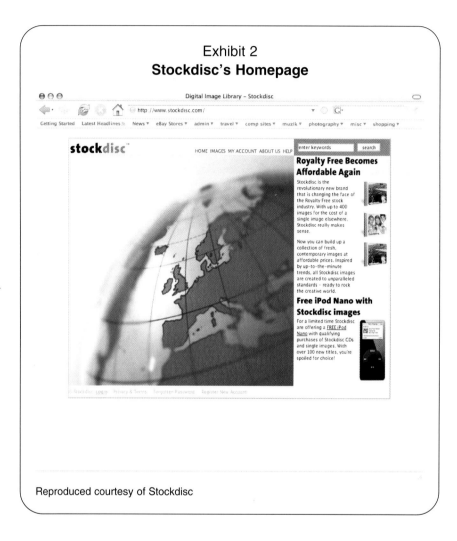

Reproduced courtesy of Stockdisc

Exhibit 3
Kerry's Eye Homepage

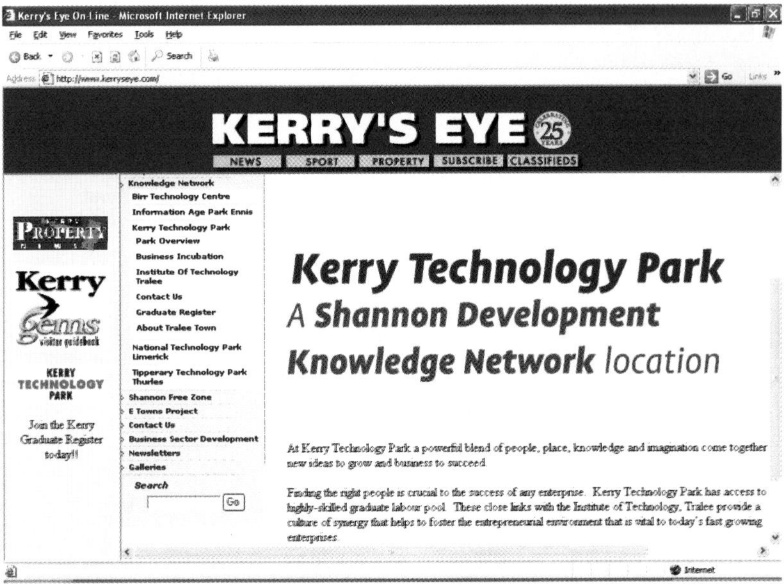

Reproduced courtesy of *Kerry's Eye*

Kevin Neville
Data Display[1]

Conor Carroll and
Naomi Birdthistle[2]

Introduction

From a small Irish rural town on the fringe of the westerly Atlantic seaboard, Data Display has been helping millions of people catch their flights, and letting them know when the next train departs and when the next blockbuster is showing at the local multiplex. Locals in Ennistymon constantly quote "next stop from here, New York". Well, that is exactly where Data Display has successfully secured a multi-million dollar contract to supply the New York Metro system with its public information displays. This company, from its humble beginnings, has built a presence on several continents and illuminated the lives of millions of people looking for information. As Kevin Neville prepares to leave Data Display's headquarters in Ennistymon, Co. Clare for a trade mission to India, he checks the designs of the firm's latest, mammoth display array that will reside in Paris's Charles de Gaulle airport terminal. With the production team he has worked with for decades, he knows all is in very capable hands as he seeks out further opportunities for Data Display in Asia. The success of Data Display is quite extraordinary. The company has already overcome numerous barriers including financial crises, rapid technological changes, a high cost base and a remote geographic location. For Kevin Neville and his team, it would seem that nothing is impossible, no challenge insurmountable. However, for this highly successful, indigenous Irish business some of the biggest challenges were yet to come.

Background to Data Display

Data Display has emerged from its humble origins to be a market leader in the design and manufacture of electronic information displays. The company was initially established back in 1979 to produce disco lights for the Irish market. Back then, Ireland was a very different place to the exuberance of the modern Celtic Tiger. Unemployment was rife, interest rates were colossal, venture capital was very difficult to raise and opportunities were few and far between. Kevin used his entrepreneurial flair to establish Textlite with the help of Dutch investors, with Kevin holding 25 per cent of the company. The company exploited the opportunity to expand into retail-type electronic signage, developing single line text display signs, particularly for the retail industry. Since then the company has grown, and now serves numerous different types of markets with customised information display solutions. Exhibits 1 and 2 help us to understand the rapid development of Data Display, and to track its international success, by illustrating key company milestones (see Exhibits 1 and 2).

The company achieved very promising sales from this initial business foray and the company was floated on the Dutch Parallel Market. However, in 1988, Kevin decided to buy out the Dutch investors. In this management buyout deal Kevin acquired ownership of the factory and its machinery. Also the Dutch holding company, under the terms of the agreement with Kevin, would not enter into direct competition for a designated period. By 1991 the company was experiencing financial turmoil, with creditors owing the company IR£1.6 million going into receivership. Banks then threatened to foreclose its loans, declaring the firm bankrupt and taking over the firm. However, personal guarantees and mortgaging all of Kevin's assets several times over gave the firm the necessary breathing space to recover. Kevin put everything on the line to overcome this financial crisis. The company took the name of Data Display and was free from the control of the then bankrupt Dutch holding company. All of the borrowings made by the firm were repaid to the banks within a three-year period. The company survived this dramatic turbulent period, and was now free to pursue its own strategy, forging ahead with its own destiny.

Kevin Neville – The Man Behind This International Success Story

Growing up in Galway, at fifteen years of age, Kevin left school and joined the army. His father, a Garda, and his mother, who was a teacher, constantly encouraged him to choose "a nice pensionable career". But Kevin felt that a tried and trusted route would simply bore him. In the army he was assigned to the Signals Corp and was then sent back to school. He completed his City & Guilds qualification in electronics in Kevin Street College (now known as DIT) and completed diplomas in the UK. He then went on to work for a company called Plassey in England as a designer, developing VHF and UHF tuners for televisions. At the age of twenty-three he got his first lucky break working for GEC, a subsidiary of General Electric UK, firstly as a technician, and then as a manager, and began to get noticed in the company with his units making profits in very difficult markets. He reorganised loss-making units, reducing costs by 25 per cent. This exemplary track record led Kevin to become manager for London, then southern England and then England as a whole, managing over 700 technicians on the road. As Kevin explains:

> I was the black sheep of the family, I didn't go to university, I did everything wrong, I ran away and joined the army at 15 years of age. But lucky enough I joined the "army signal corp." and they sent me back to school.

He had become noticed by GEC's chairman Arnold Winestock, one of Britain's foremost industrialists. GEC was one of Britain's largest and most successful companies, and became the first ever British company to break the STG£1 billion profit barrier. Kevin sees Arnold Winestock as the person who really inspired him in business, by his "no nonsense results-driven approach". The industrialist wouldn't tolerate excuses from his staff. This is where Kevin cut his teeth in management. His experience within GEC gave Kevin solid experience not only in management dealing with unions, but in sales also. He found his time in GEC a fantastic experience, where he constantly learned from those around him. He was involved in numerous GEC projects, such as productivity initiatives and various company acquisitions. At this time Kevin's meteoric performance was even being noticed elsewhere, with companies attempting to head-hunt him. He spent over fifteen years within GEC, working mainly in the UK, but also on the continent for a number of years working on several GEC projects.

Eventually Kevin relented to the phone calls from headhunters, and took up an offer from a German electronics firm wanting to set up a manufacturing operation in Ireland. Kevin wanted to move back to Ireland because he wanted to bring up his family back home. Moving back represented a big risk for Kevin: a wage cut, forsaking a possible directorship within GEC and launching a high-risk start-up. The German multinational wanted an Irish manufacturing base due to the low wage cost infrastructure prevalent at the time. Kevin not only established a manufacturing capability, but a strong research and development team. Within the first six months the company was making over half a million pounds in profit, and every penny of that went back to Germany. Subsequent profits went in a similar direction. The multinational company had a beautiful new factory in Ennis, with substantial governmental support. The company, at this stage, was employing over 700 people, making it one of Ireland's largest employers at the time, and exporting over IR£20 million worth of product. However, Kevin was extremely unhappy with the German parent company's lack of support for the Irish operation: none of the profits were being reinvested in the Irish operations, but were simply being repatriated to Germany, despite higher productivity rates than in other manufacturing centres. Kevin vividly recalls handing over large cheques to German executives, and getting a simple "thank you" in return, and nothing else. Relations became fraught and he felt he was not benefiting from all of his hard work. He felt this enterprise was not going in a viable direction; the parent company was simply exploiting a cheap workforce, and was not investing in the company. In the run up to Christmas, he handed in his notice and the keys to his company car. What now?

Winestock, his business mentor for over fifteen years, had offered him the opportunity to return to GEC if things didn't work out. Kevin decided to take the plunge and remain on in Ireland. He had developed a basic product, which he sought to manufacture. The product was a basic discotheque lights product, which consisted of three lights with three different filters that could be placed beside a speaker. Bands like Boney M and the Bee Gees were in vogue. Government agencies offered Kevin numerous sites as possible starting points for the venture, all based in small rural towns on the periphery, including Achill Island and the Gaeltacht, and, finally, Ennistymon was chosen. Furthermore they were offering numerous incentives to start up a manufacturing enterprise in remote, rural locations. The factory was originally a metal manufacturing firm that had gone bankrupt. Kevin thought this was the type of facility he needed for his new venture, and he didn't want to uproot his family once again.

In those early heady days, the company hired thirteen women to initially assemble and manufacture the disco lights product. Kevin used his industry contacts to get key orders from retailers such as Boots and Dixons. Kevin knew that the product's life cycle would reach its end fairly shortly. He focused on the company's resources and on the types of products that would best suit the business, such as developing remote controls and LED (Light Emitting Diode) displays. From there he went on to develop a range of products with the help of his Dutch investors. Kevin had invested his life, all his assets and mortgaged his house to make sure the business stayed afloat. He was continually in survival mode for his Data Display business, continually striving for new business opportunities. Breaking into crucial export markets was vital for his business to succeed. Some of the company's original success was down to entering new markets with low cost products. In one case, Kevin and his team went to a Chicago trade exhibition with one of his new display products. Advisors from the Irish Trade Board were wary that the company was out of its depth in the market. They were advised to go home. The advisor from the Irish Export Board soon changed his mind when he saw similar competing products on sale in nearby stands for $2,500, while Data Display products were on sale for $600–$1,000. He returned to their stand and said, "lads you're on to a winner here." The company has now evolved considerably and serves multiple markets such as traffic, passenger information, commercial/retail, industrial, financial and entertainment (see Exhibit 3), as Kevin explains:

> You have to look internationally; we're such a small market here, that you can't have a manufacturing plant in Ireland unless you have, like us, 90 per cent or even 100 per cent of its manufacturing going overseas.

DATA DISPLAY'S PRODUCTS AND MANUFACTURING PROCESS

It would be wrong to envisage Data Display as just a simple manufacturing company, producing an array of products for industrial clients. Data Display is a solution-driven company rather than a product company. When a potential client comes to Data Display with a problem, the company develops a customised solution to that problem. For example, the firm's research and development (R&D) section would develop a customised design solution for a particular customer matching their particular specifications. Customised management software would be developed for the particular client (e.g. a cinema chain required software that would display information over the auditorium, the screens and outdoors). The company has created highly customised products for its client base, with numerous value-added benefits for customers. For example, one of its products has an inbuilt diagnostics system that will identify problems within the system to a controller, down to the exact location of a fault (e.g. one faulty LED on a display array). This type of value-added mechanism allows clients to repair quickly and cost effectively, causing minimal disruption.

The firm's entire state-of-the-art production facility is computer networked, enabling the sales order to be tracked throughout its life cycle. This allows the firm to have a high level of control. Over the years, the plant has been significantly revamped and extended to cope with additional demands. Every inch of the manufacturing floor space is used, for fabrication, assembly, painting and testing of products.

Data Display has invested substantially in research and development, so that its products are at the cutting edge in terms of display solutions, with substantial money being ploughed back into the business to fund R&D and the purchase of robotic assembly machines. The company has a team of twenty-eight engineers in R&D. Over 11 per cent of revenues are continually reinvested into research within the company. By ensuring that the company has a strong in-house R&D capability, Data Display is focusing on staying one step ahead of the competition. Furthermore, the company has developed a world-class manufacturing plant that allows it to use state-of-the-art machinery to facilitate the development of customised display solutions. Exhibit 4 shows Data Display's headquarters in Ennistymon.

108

The Sales Process

A large portion of the business is derived from successfully obtaining public tenders. A team within Data Display sits down and works out a bid proposal. The team includes design engineers, sales and the firm's cost accountant. The entire bid is costed out in finite detail. The team then looks at possible threats, i.e. who is going to compete with their bid, what will they be offering, what can they offer. All of these variables have to be taken into account. In some instances international sales offices may have to forego their sales margin as the tender is too competitive and the contract may be critical for the business in gaining extra sales from the client in the future. In some instances Data Display has been beaten to contracts by a low-priced competing bid. In this instance, a competitor would price their proposal at a ridiculously low price, promise brilliant after sales service, and then fail to deliver on these promises when there is a fault with the product. Some competitors are desperate to secure a contract, pricing the tender at below costs, and knowing well that it is impossible to service. Politics can come into play within tendering processes, as the decision-makers are guided by consultants and experts with allegiances to particular companies. Exhibit 5 illustrates Data Display's main competitors.

Customisation is one of the firm's biggest strengths. Through its R&D team the firm can design, manufacture and install any display solution that the customer requires. The company finds that its competitors cannot compete with this key dynamic. Competitors would offer a display product, of a specified specification, with limited flexibility. However Data Display could offer the customer what they wanted in terms of size, shape, weight and particular features that the customer required, at a reasonable cost. This was one of the main reasons why Data Display secured the New York Metro contract. Customisation is offered to any client, but now that the company has a large portfolio of products in its portfolio, it encourages its sales team to use an array of options within the product catalogue. If customers want a fully customised product, Data Display has additional costs that have to be met, including development, tooling and engineering costs. In order to successfully obtain a customer's order, the firm consults closely with the client on its exact design needs. In some cases, this can be a very protracted consultation process involving architects, engineers and committees. In some cases, customers would demand a working sample or prototype in very short lead times to convince them of Data Display's capability.

The firm has now built up a wealth of experience and expertise in delivering display solutions to international clients. With over twenty-five years of experience, the firm is well equipped to deal with any customer's display problem. In the rail sector, it has over fifteen years of experience, which brings with it a vast knowledge about the industry and its particular needs. In promoting the business the company relies on trade shows, direct mail shots, its website (which are all country specific) and the support of Enterprise Ireland in new emerging markets such as Poland, India, Belgium and Switzerland. As Kevin comments:

> There is no point in going into a country unless you know who is in there, what you are going to be up against, what's their strengths, their weaknesses, how are you going to attack them.

THE BIG SALE

One of the key breaks for the business was to get into the multiplex cinema market, which happened serendipitously as this new phenomenon took off worldwide. The company made initial contact with Warner Bros., who owned a chain of international cinemas. The company got an order to fit out the display systems for a new multiplex in Australia. The client was impressed, particularly the chairman, and the company secured a raft of orders for the UK, where Warner Bros. were expanding quite aggressively, opening over forty cinemas. In order to get this business, Kevin flew over to New York on several occasions to make a pitch for the business. This involved waiting and waiting to get an opportunity to talk to the chairman outside his office. Eventually Kevin got his opportunity. As the chairman was leaving his office, Kevin asked for five minutes of his time, referring to the chariman's initial interest in the product. "You wonder how you get markets like that", says Kevin. "Sweat and blood I tell you. It's hard."

His opening gambit paid off as the chain agreed to view a prototype of an integrated cinema system. Kevin and his Data Display team flew over a working prototype to New York, and demonstrated the product, which could be successfully integrated with the cinema's own management software. Persistence and determination won the day as Kevin secured orders for his products for Warner Bros.' cinemas in several international markets, and in the USA. Getting into the cinema market was a huge step forward for the company. The company installed its products in high pro-file locations such as in Leicester Square in London. This created a domino effect in that other cinema chains began to take notice. Having cracked Warner Bros. and having installed displays in flagship locations, the company went on to secure major deals with Viacom's National Amusements, which operates Showcase Cinemas, Multiplex Cinemas, and Cinema de Lux with about 1,425 screens across the US, Europe and Latin America. For every new multiplex that opened, it gave Data Display a potential revenue stream. The Data Display team would attend every new multiplex opening, ensuring that things went off without a hitch. This level of personal service led to solidifying hard-won business relationships with clients. If it missed one opening, it was gone! Everything had to be all right on the night. Now the firm has performed installations in Japan and Korea. Kevin recollects with fondness the gala opening of a new multiplex in London's West End, where he was climbing a ladder before the glitzy premiere of a Hollywood blockbuster in his tuxedo, personally ensuring that the installation was okay.

Getting a large blue chip customer advocate that can be used as a reference is vital in securing the confidence of large companies. These reputations are hard earned and take enormous groundwork to develop. For instance, a prospective US-based client would ask, "what does your company produce? Where is the company based? How do you know about my market? What are my needs? Who are your company's customers?" When you are a small Irish company based in a small town in the west of Ireland, you need to build a solid reputation that will win over the confidence and trust of clients.

INTERNATIONALISATION STRATEGY

Initially Data Display used a number of foreign distributors/agents to gain access to overseas markets. These agents typically had the contacts, as well as the experience in dealing with large accounts, such as transport networks. An opportunity arose in the early 1990s for Data Display to buy its UK distributor. The original company had gone bankrupt, so Kevin bought the company, which had great industry contacts with large clients, like the London Underground. Initially, the company used trade fairs as its prime marketing activity in getting overseas orders, such as the Hanover Fair in Germany. At some trade fairs Kevin and his team would come back with a full order book for the year. These trade shows were intense experiences, a full week of pitching and negotiating for business. One of Data Display's core strengths is its ability to provide customised solutions for its clients. If a customer doesn't like the size of a product, Data Display could react and offer the client an alternative quickly and cheaply. For instance initially the company did business in the US through a distributor. However if the customer had a problem Data Display would then deal directly with the customer on a solution. Distributors felt that this was eroding their role and negating their control in the process.

However, for Data Display to operate effectively, direct access was crucial in order to understand exactly what the customer required and to deliver a flexible, customised solution. Closeness to the customer incurred greater costs, but led to greater customer insight, customised service delivery and ultimately strengthening the business relationship with the end customer. With such a small domestic market, Data Display had to look at export markets. Data Display set up its first international sales office in Holland; a surprising choice as, for many Irish manufacturers, the UK seems like the obvious choice for a firm tentatively starting to export abroad. This sales office was set up in 1991 with Dutch partners. The international sales offices have emerged incrementally, through a series of joint ventures, partnerships and buyouts. For instance, Data Display Sweden is 40 per cent owned by the company, with the Swedish management team owning 20 per cent of the business. Through this strategy Data Display has gained from accessing local management's business acumen and contacts, incentivising local management and gaining control over local subsidiaries' activities. Data Display UK was initially a competing organisation. However Kevin acquired 50 per cent of the business, later going on to acquire a further 40 per cent and eventually buying out the original partners. The UK sales office now employs twenty-two employees. Ever vigilant for an opportunity, Kevin bought its Portuguese operations for €1, but assumed all of the company's liabilities. If a competitor or distributor went bankrupt, the company moved quickly to assess possibilities. By doing so the company gained access to key government contracts such as the London Underground. These were no easy decisions, as taking over a company would mean that the company would assume responsibility for maintenance contracts. This exploited opportunity lead to the acquisition of further rail contracts.

Over 86 per cent of the company's sales come through the firm's own sales offices. Having a direct sales force enables the firm to have more control over selling activity. Management has ownership over salesperson quality and their performance. Activities such as customer service and marketing can be coordinated more effectively. As a result, Data Display has full customer ownership and can build and nurture customer relationships and has total control over customer experience. The company has used indirect channels initially to gain access to foreign markets to see the viability of that foreign market, before establishing a more direct sales channel, through buying out distributors or forming joint partnerships. In some instances, an indirect partner has capabilities that are very hard to replicate. Also they can be useful if there is a need to gain rapid entry into a market to achieve wider geographic coverage and limit risk exposure. Every Monday morning there is a top management team meeting, to discuss the production and sales situation. Then in the afternoon all of the subsidiaries report to Kevin via a teleconference on progress and key issues. Each month all of the subsidiaries prepare a status report for the sales and marketing director. Having a presence in multiple international markets and within different industry sectors insulates the company from sudden downturns in demand from particular markets, as Kevin explains:

> I'm now dealing direct with the end customer and I know what that customer wants and I can go back, design it and I can now reduce my design costs because I got direct access to the end customer. Secondly I know what the customer wants and likes and dislikes by getting direct feedback from the market, which I couldn't get back through my dealer.

Data Display now has a formal management structure, with Kevin acting as both managing director and chairman. The three main divisions of the company are production, R&D, and sales and marketing. The company is now 100 per cent privately owned by the Neville family after they successfully bought it back from investors. Kevin's family have become actively involved in the management and operation of the company. Paul, his eldest son, has taken on the role as sales and marketing director, while Kevin's daughter and son-in-law head up the US sales office. Another sibling is not involved in the business – "the clever one, perhaps", comments Kevin.

CHALLENGES FOR DATA DISPLAY

Like many other Irish firms, Data Display faces a number of challenges. In the globalised business environment, Data Display experiences downward pressure on price because of competition from low cost countries. In some instances, Data Display has installed a number of its products in Asian countries, only to find the displays badly copied and installed by local manufacturers cloning Data Display's products. Customers are becoming more demanding in terms of cost and extra services. There are no rules for competition, since products have to be elevated above being seen as basic commodities where price is the sole determinant in the consumer's buying criteria. In order to compete successfully, companies have to strive for sustainable competitive advantage through both product and process excellence.

Technological advances have brought tremendous changes to the industry, particularly in the areas of automation and manufacturing. At one point, Data Display employed 360 people installing components by hand. Now the company has highly sophisticated, state-of-the-art machinery that installs over 50,000 components in an instant. One of the biggest challenges for the business is to keep abreast of the rapid technology changes. For instance, for internal installations, customers want displays on both wide and plasma screens. Now the latest customer demand is LCD (Liquid Crystal Display) screens or TFT (Thin Film Transistor) displays. Now the company can provide a wide range of different display options dependent on customer demands, whether it is a TFT, LCD or LED display. The company has the manufacturing capability, the majority of which is in-house. One of the major strengths of the company is being agile enough to react to whatever the customer wants. One of the biggest advantages for Data Display is that it has an international direct sales force, which constantly feeds the management team with the latest market trends and pertinent market intelligence. This invaluable feedback mechanism allows the firm to adapt to changing market needs, and adjust and enhance its product offerings.

Data Display creates displays that are highly reliable and durable, rugged to withstand the most rigorous of quality standards. These displays are housed in custom-made casings that have to withstand vandals and exacting fire safety standards. For example a display screen for an underground rail network must be halogen-free, mustn't burn, mustn't give off any fumes and must withstand the diesel fumes. Normal consumer screens used in domestic markets could not withstand these challenges, and would break down in a couple of weeks. The marketplace is constantly evolving due to technology. Markets are being created in new sectors that were previously unviable and not technically feasible. For example, with outdoor advertising, the costs of installing a high impact display suitable for advertising have fallen dramatically. Now these displays can be powered through low cost solar energy units and the content can be managed remotely through 3G mobile technologies. Technology advancements provide both new opportunities and threats for the business.

Operating in such a remote, beautiful location has its advantages and notable drawbacks. The company has an intensely loyal and dedicated workforce, which are focused on ensuring Data Display's success, as there are limited job opportunities in a small town such as Ennistymon. Eleven employees have been with the company for over twenty-one years, and fourteen have been with the company for over fifteen years. The company also operates a profit share scheme, so that 10 per cent of the profits are given back to employees. The company doesn't have a trade union, but it does have a works committee. The factory in itself is one of the company's most powerful selling tools. Potential clients are invited to the factory, where there is a hive of activity, showcasing the plant's excellent manufacturing capability. On the downside, coordinating an international sales effort from the periphery of Europe presents unique challenges for the firm. Data Display is heavily reliant on international flights to and from Shannon to conduct international business. However, the company has had to use, with increased frequency, routes originating from Dublin airport. This involves a four-and-a-half-hour drive to Dublin airport. To operate a world-class manufacturing factory in Ireland can prove costly, due to high labour, insurance and freight costs in comparison to other locations. Many commentators within Ireland see the indigenous manufacturing industry as unsustainable due to competition from low cost countries.

Some international sales offices proved less than fruitful. For example, in 1996 the company set up Data Display Germany, which was expected to be a major source of new business for the firm. However, recession in Germany following reunification led to poor sales. A decision had to be made whether to continue having a physical presence in the country. Kevin made the decision that enough was enough and that the operation had to close down. He gave his German employees the option of a Data Display agency, where they could work for themselves. This proved to be a more sustainable option, as this operation was haemorrhaging money.

Similarly, the company founded a US sales office with a US-based partner. It envisaged having two sales offices, one in LA (this is where the cinema chains were based) and one in New York. Over a period of time, the LA office was losing money, and not justifying its existence. The staff were possibly too accustomed to the easygoing Californian lifestyle. The New York office initially proved successful, generating sizeable revenue streams. However Kevin became weary of his business partner, as the firm's strategy was continually failing to be implemented. In the aftermath of the September 11 attacks sales plunged from €10 million to €2 million, with all of the subsidiary's failings being blamed on this tragic event. Kevin had enough, bought out his local partner and sacked the original US team. His daughter, who at the time was managing the Dublin sales office, volunteered to head up a completely new sales office in New York. Since then there has been a complete reversal and the US represents Data Display's brightest growth prospect.

The sales teams work on 8–10 per cent commission of the margin earned on a sales order. Now the company is also focusing on securing the maintenance contracts of key installations. On numerous occasions the company has been called in to rectify problems of competitors' products. The company now sees this as a lucrative revenue stream, selling ten-year maintenance contracts for display systems. The firm will look after the whole life cycle cost.

THE NEXT STEP

Data Display is now at a crossroads. Kevin, its founder, is thinking about handing over the reins of the company to the younger generation of Nevilles. The company is in the black, having repaid the bank all of its borrowings; it nearly faced financial obliteration twice, when creditors went bankrupt. The company has established an excellent international sales network, which is continually feeding the manufacturing plant in Ennistymon with busy production schedules. Kevin sees that the company has a number of options: pursuing the status quo, raising additional capital, floating the company on the stock exchange, or even selling it outright. When Kevin eventually calls it a day he knows that his company – a company he has helped craft into a tremendous success story – will still thrive under the reins of his family and his excellent management team. He feels that the success of the company is not all down to him, but to the excellent team within the company. Some of his staff have been with the company for years, taking part in Data Display's exciting international journey. His other major interest outside of business is horse breeding, to which he wants to dedicate more time when he eventually retires. Asked whether entrepreneurs are made or born, Kevin believes it is the hunger to succeed that drives business success. He believes that fear of failure is the primary motivator that has helped him succeed. The company has even bigger and brighter ideas as it moves forward, as Kevin explains:

> The only thing is to be enthusiastic about it and say –
> "I'm going to do this!" Think about it as best you can, but
> make the decision to move. I've been asked the question
> "what makes an entrepreneur?" – he does something. He
> doesn't sit around talking about it; he just does it.

As Kevin departs for his flight to Bombay, seeking out new opportunities with the same enthusiasm he had thirty years ago, he looks back with tremendous pride on the Ennistymon plant he created, which now employs 130 staff. He knows Data Display has a number of new challenges, yet as he has shown in the past, nothing is impossible, and every obstacle can be overcome. In beating the competition, Kevin has always followed a basic mantra – "produce it quicker, cheaper and better than the competition, offering customised solutions backed up with excellent customer service".

As technology continually changes the firm has to successfully adjust to the new global competitive landscape these shifts bring. For Data Display to continue to be successful, it must meet the needs of the changing market. Competing internationally from a location on the periphery of

Europe is proving increasingly difficult. The cost advantages of manufacturing in Ireland are being continually eroded by competition from low cost manufacturing countries. Sustaining the firm's competitive advantage over rivals is essential if it is to win new orders and maintain relations with existing clients. The level of flexibility and customisation that Data Display can provide customers has proved to be a winning formula, yet maintaining these traits is a key managerial challenge for the firm. Managing, motivating and controlling the company's diverse international operations is of paramount importance. The key challenge for Kevin and Data Display is to ensure that the business continues to grow after Kevin eventually decides to hang up his sales suit. For many businesses, a core obstacle is ensuring the continued success of the business once the drive and energy of the company's founder departs. In some cases, their personality shapes the business, and is an integral part of the firm's culture. Therein lies the key challenge for any entrepreneurial business – laying the foundations for the continued success of the business – in Data Display's case, possibly without Kevin at the helm.

NOTES

1   This case was prepared by Conor Carroll and Dr Naomi Birdthistle as the basis for class discussion rather than to illustrate either effective or ineffective handling of a business situation.

2   Conor Carroll lectures in Marketing, and Naomi Birdthistle lectures in Entrepreneurship at the University of Limerick (conor.carroll@ul.ie; naomi.birdthistle@ul.ie). The authors are extremely grateful to Kevin Neville for his time and his inspiration in helping to prepare this case.

Exhibit 1
Key Company Milestones

1979	**Set up as Textlite** Initially sold disco lights to Irish market. Company 75 per cent owned by Dutch investors and 25 per cent owned by Kevin Neville.
1985	**Textlite floated on Dutch Parallel Market** The company was very successfully floated as Textlite Holdings NV.
1988	**Management buyout by Kevin Neville** Kevin acquired the factory and machinery as result of the buyout.
1991	**Set-up of Data Display** Following a turbulent period, Textlite was renamed Data Display, with the company free to pursue its own strategy.
1992	**Set-up of Data Display UK** Kevin personally set up a Data Display sales office in the UK.
1993	**ISO Certification** Gained ISO9001 recognition for its production facilities.
1995	**ICC Bank takes a substantial stake** ICC Bank (now Bank of Scotland Ireland) takes a 20 per cent stake in the business, providing much needed capital investment to facilitate expansion.
1996	**Takeover of IGG (UK) and Eridan (France) and set-up of Data Display USA** IGG successfully purchased, giving the company greater access to the UK market and expertise with the rail sector. Eridan, originally Data Display's French distributor, bought out using a share swap. Another share swap helped create Data Display USA with a business partner.

1998	**Set-up of Data Display Netherlands and Data Display Portugal** Through a joint venture Data Display Netherlands was created. In Portugal a local distributor, Apadil, was taken over and renamed Data Display Portugal.
1999	**New factory opens and further consolidation** New 60,000 sq.ft. production facility in Ennistymon opens.
2001	**Investment in Poltech, Sweden** Acquires Poltech in a joint venture with its Swedish distributor, giving the company additional manufacturing resources and access to a strong customer portfolio.
2004	**Bought PD Systems** Purchase of PD Systems allows the firm to manufacture TFT monitors, which are suitable for bus, rail and airport markets. Previously these important products had to be outsourced from several suppliers.
2005	**Re-purchase of Data Display shares** Company repurchases all shares, the company is now 100 per cent owned by the Neville family.

Exhibit 2
Data Display – At a Glance

Background
➤ Owner – Kevin Neville ➤ Founded in 1979 ➤ Designs and manufactures customised electronic information displays ➤ Employs 130 employees in Ennistymon and over 100 staff in international sales offices ➤ Generates nearly €20 million a year in revenue ➤ *"Europe's Leading Supplier of Electronic Information Displays"*

Location of Data Display
➤ Data Display headquarters is based in the picturesque town of Ennistymon, Co. Clare. Ennistymon is a small town on Ireland's westerly seaboard. Data Display is the town's largest employer. Approximately 263 km from Dublin.

Location of Data Display Sales Offices	Clients Include:
Data Display USA	New York Metro
Data Display UK	Warner Cinemas
Data Display Ireland	Charles de Gaulle Airport
Data Display France	Heathrow Express
Data Display Netherlands	London Underground
Data Display Portugal	Copenhagen Stock Exchange
Data Display Sweden (TA Poltech)	National Amusements
Data Display Australia	Seattle Light Rail

Types of Products Sold	Markets Include:
LCD Display Signs	Public Transport – Rail & Bus
Datalines (single line text/scrolling or static)	Road
	Airports
Data Boards	Banks
TFT Displays	Cinemas
Reception Displays	Call Centres
Advertising Displays	Shopping Centres
Ticker Displays	Forecourt Stations
Forecourt Petrol Displays	Hotels & Conference Centres
Large Departure Boards	Leisure Parks & Stadia
Large Highway Signs	Municipalities
	Banks
	Stock Markets

Exhibit 3
Examples of Data Display's Product Range

Cinema Displays

Passenger Information
– Rail Network

Traffic Information
– Road Signage

Stock Exchange Information Display

Petrol Forecourt – Information Signage

Stock Ticker Information Display

Exhibit 4
Data Display's Ennistymon Headquarters

Exhibit 5
Data Display's Main Competitors

Daktronics Inc.	Vossloh Information Technologies GmbH	Mitron OY
Based in South Dakota, USA	Based in Kiel, Germany	Based in Forssa, Finland.
www.daktronics.com	www.vit.vossloh.com	www.mitron.fi
Varied product range includes: scoreboards, commercial and advertising, financial, traffic, cinema/entertainment, passenger information, parking.	Specialises in technology systems for rail-bound transport including display products.	Product range includes: public transport passenger information displays and media measurement systems. Also provides signs for petrol stations, traffic and ports.
Established in 1968. Manufacturer. 1,800 people employed. Became a publicly traded company in 1994 on the NASDAQ. Technologies include: LED, LCD and video products. Sales for the nine months to end Jan 2006 is US$219m.	20 years in the business. Owned by the large multinational Vossloh Group. Has 300 employees. Technologies: LCD, TFT, VFD, LED and electromechanical. Locations include: Kiel, Berlin, Munich, New York, Zurich, Vienna, Malmö, Budapest and Hangzhou.	Founded in 1988. Particularly strong in Scandinavian markets. Technologies: LCD, TFT and stationary displays.

Trans Lux Corp.	Densitron/Ferrograph	Solari di Udine S.p.A.
Based in Connecticut & Iowa, USA	Based in Newcastle-upon-Tyne, UK.	Based in Udine, Italy
www.trans-lux.com	www.densitron.com/ferrograph	www.solari.it
Product range includes: indoor and outdoor displays, scoreboards, passenger information, advertising and cinema displays.	Product range includes: passenger information, media, call centres and rear projection displays for cinemas.	Product range includes: passenger information, traffic/parking, advertising, clocks, time attendance and access control.
Established in 1920. Listed on the American Stock Exchange since 1925. Originally a cinema chain owner. Pioneered many leading technologies. Technologies: LED, LCD, Plasma and Video.	Established since 1985. Combined with Densitron. Its products are sold under the Ferrograph name. Listed on the London stock exchange. Specialises in technologies such as: LED, LCD, TFT and Plasma.	Founded in 1948. Has 250 employees. Technologies: LED, LCD, flip dot, CRT monitors, plasma and TFT.

Diarmuid Hegarty
Griffith College Dublin[1]

GERALDINE MCGING AND
PAULINE CONNOLLY[2]

INTRODUCTION

It is Monday morning and Diarmuid Hegarty, Chairman of Griffith College Dublin (GCD), is preparing for the monthly board meeting with the company's directors. Sitting at his desk, he leans back on his chair and begins to reflect on how a college with over 7,000 students and an international campus in Moscow developed out of such humble beginnings. There is no doubt that Griffith College has come a long way. Its facilities at Griffith Barracks are a far cry from the makeshift classroom that was Diarmuid's parents' dinning room back in the early 1970s. Situated on a seven-acre campus within a mile of St Stephen's Green on Dublin's South Circular Road, Griffith College is currently Ireland's largest independent third level educational provider.

The transformation has not been easy. Diarmuid has had to deal with a series of crises, none of which could have been anticipated, but any one of which could have brought his company to its knees. Diarmuid and his team have not only overcome these crises, but they have also managed to strengthen Griffith College's market position in the process.

As he casts his eye over the agenda for the meeting, Diarmuid focuses on items 3: Future Strategy, and 4: Succession Planning. The higher education sector is becoming increasingly competitive, particularly at the international level where everyone is trying to get a slice of the overseas market. If Griffith College is to retain its position as market leader it will have to adopt a new strategic approach, and this will inevitably mean changes. In addition, while Diarmuid is the founding entrepreneur of this successful educational venture, he will not always be at the helm. When will be the right time for his role in this particular entrepreneurial roller-coaster journey to come to an end? Just as he is deep in thought, his phone rings. He grabs his Board papers and puts them into his brief case. "I'm on my way", he says.

DIARMUID HEGARTY – BACKGROUND OF THE ENTREPRENEUR

Diarmuid Hegarty (see Exhibit 1) comes from an affluent, coastal Dublin suburb. He graduated in 1972 as an accountant and started a potentially successful career as a tax consultant with Coopers & Lybrand where he took his "articles". Simultaneously he pursued legal studies and was later called to the Bar. He never practised law however, but instead put all his energy and enthusiasm into his accountancy career. While working for Coopers & Lybrand he became aware that accountancy students had difficulties accessing relevant study material that could assist them in passing their examinations. At that time, availability of tuition in this field was limited and was only provided on an informal basis by other accountants. Diarmuid began delivering classes to accountancy students at his parents' dining-room table and during the winter of 1972, fifteen students attended his classes. In an interview[3] with the case authors, Diarmuid explained:

> There was such a demand for the classes I eventually had to rent space away from home. By 1975, 500 students wanted tuition. Effectively, it got to a point where I had to decide in early '75 whether my career lay in tax with one of the major accounting firms or whether it lay in teaching. I made a conscious decision in spring 1975 and from 1st July we went full-time.

Although Diarmuid had secure employment and a lucrative career with a large accountancy firm, he could see the benefit of embarking on his entrepreneurial journey because the potential earning capacity of his new business was, at that time, greater than the earnings of a tax manager or junior partner. But money was not the only deciding factor, as Diarmuid explained:

> I distinctly remember asking myself whether in thirty years time I would prefer to look back on the ten sections of the Finance Acts that I had found my way around, or would I like to be able to look back at the long-term satisfaction that teaching gave me. Looking back now, I have no regrets when I see what Griffith has become, and in terms of the contribution Griffith has made to people's lives. I would say it has surpassed my expectations, and that's because of the work of a whole team of people. I also feel that if you're in education it's a vocation, but unless you are working for the State it has to be first and foremost a business.

Despite his professional qualifications, Diarmuid describes himself firstly as an educator and secondly as a businessman. During his career he lectured in University College Dublin (UCD) and the Irish Management Institute (IMI) and was a member of the Council of the Institute of Chartered Accountants in Ireland. He also served as Chairman of that Institute's Accounting Review Committee, and the Inflation Accounting Committee of the Consultative Committee of Accountancy Bodies – Ireland (CCABI). Diarmuid represented Ireland on the Accounting Standards Committee and was also chairperson of the Parliamentary & Law Committee of CCAB–Ireland. He is Chairperson of the Higher Education Colleges Association (HECA), Chairperson of the Friends of the Vocal Arts, Chairperson of the Las Adelfas Hotel partnership and Vice-Chairperson of the Ireland–Pakistan Business Council. The government of Pakistan appointed him as Honorary Consul in 2002. As well as having a dynamic personality and enjoying the sense of drama that business dealings can create, Diarmuid can also see opportunities where others do not and he tends not to adhere to recognised norms. He says of his success:

> I saw promise where others would not even have seen a flicker of potential, and I am on constant alert to identify new areas of development. I am a networker and am good

129

at pulling together resources and contacts to enable success to take place. I have great respect for the team associated with the success of Griffith; without them, it simply would not have happened.

THE DEVELOPMENT OF GRIFFITH COLLEGE

In 1978 Diarmuid formed a company called Business and Accounting Training (BAT). He remarked that:

> While the potential earning capacity of running the accountancy classes was greater than what I was earning in Deloitte, it was not the main decision-making factor in my choice to leave the company. I wanted to work for myself. I was tired of working for others, I was tired of filling out a time sheet – I hated time sheets. I wanted to be the boss and be in control of my own destiny.

In 1991, BAT acquired Griffith Barracks for €2.5 million. This site was chosen because it was large enough to accommodate substantial expansion in the future. Today the site houses the restored historic buildings, a modern accommodation block and a state-of-the-art conference centre with all supporting facilities (see Exhibit 2). Griffith continued its expansion and now has campuses in Cork and Limerick. Courses are also delivered in Waterford, Ennis and Moscow, and an office has been established in Beijing. The campus that operated in Karachi is now being wound down as it was proving to be a financial challenge to the company. Diarmuid is proud of the success of Griffith students and says, "our excellent student pass rates are reinforced by the many national prizes students have received".

THE GRIFFITH MANAGEMENT TEAM

Griffith College is currently owned by three shareholders: Diarmuid Hegarty is Executive Chairman of Bellerophon, trading as Griffith College, and is the majority shareholder of the company with 65 per cent of the shares; Reginald Callanan, who has taught alongside Diarmuid since 1982, holds 30 per cent of the shares; and Pierce Kent, who joined BAT in 1978, holds 5 per cent. The company is managed by a Board of Directors that includes the shareholders. Tomás MacEochagain is the Managing Director, and Leo O'Brien, Frank Scott-Lennon, Philip Burke and Ronan Fenlon are Directors on the Board. The Board of Management comprises Diarmuid Hegarty, Reg Callanan, Tomás MacEochagain, Leo O'Brien, Philip Burke, Ronan Fenlon and Pat Sheehan. Each faculty within the college is managed by a course director who reports to the Board of Management.

It is interesting to note how the management team was actually selected. Particular individuals were invited onto the Board because of their contribution to the college at critical stages in its development. In his interview with the case authors, Diarmuid frequently mentioned that the college owes its success to the teamwork of those involved, as each person brings a unique set of skills to the table. According to Diarmuid, the Board members have demonstrated a long-term commitment to the college and their contribution would make a huge difference to the college across different key areas:

> Unquestionable entrepreneurial success can only be achieved as a result of team effort. At the end of the day, every team has to have a driver. One quality that has contributed to our success is the openness of the team. Sometimes we thrash something out and sometimes we do something without hesitation, provided we are confident it will work. Basically, if someone comes up with a crazy idea that hasn't a chance, they will be told so. But, if one of us comes up with a crazy idea that really has potential, then it will be thrashed out, the risks will be limited and a strategy will be developed to run with it. We have more freedom now to run with new courses and develop new campuses than we had ten years ago when we were strapped for cash. Now, as a result of our recent expansion, we have to tighten our belts, which can sometimes set new expansion plans back two or three years because we can only incur capital expenditure in digestible lumps.

Interestingly, all the members of the management team at Griffith College are male, all are white and all are Irish – facts that have not escaped Diarmuid's attention:

> Sometimes we are criticised for our all-male member-ship. But my view is that there is no point in having female Board members just for the sake of gender bal-ance. Any new Board member will need to offer the same level of commitment as existing members, and will be expected to contribute in a way that will enhance the future of the college's success.

EARLY CRISES

Reg Callanan joined Griffith in 1982, and has been a key player in deal-ing with crises. 1983 saw the company face one of its first major chal-lenges: the Chartered Public Accountants (CPA) that approved the courses delivered by BAT decided they would no longer verify these courses. If the approving body no longer verified the courses, the com-pany had no product to sell and, therefore, would have to wind down its operations. Callanan, who later became a shareholder in the company, suggested to Diarmuid that, rather than face defeat and unemployment, BAT should consider delivering courses validated by the Association of Chartered Certified Accountants (ACCA). This turned out to be an enlightened proposal and the college is today viewed as one of the best ACCA accountancy colleges in the world, with Griffith's students having been awarded both national and international prizes in professional accountancy examinations.

The company faced its second major crisis in September 1992, when there was a currency crisis in Ireland. As interest rates rose, property prices fell. The company was under enormous financial strain and there was also a fall in the current asset value of the site, as Reg[4] recalls:

> At times the bank balance was under enormous pressure with bills mounting up and salaries needing to be paid. We had to be financially creative in order to meet the company's commitments and did this by prioritising our obligations. Firstly, wages had to be paid, followed by the

mortgage and then the utilities. The building refurbishment programme had to be curtailed and the plan to construct student accommodation was deferred indefinitely.

The company decided to concentrate its limited financial resources on the refurbishment of the listed buildings that were in a serious state of disrepair.

Tomás MacEochagain[5] joined Griffith College in the late 1980s. His primary role was to source new business and to develop a computing faculty. He embraced this challenge with enthusiasm and that faculty is now very successful. There was great demand for computing degrees during the 1990s, resulting in large numbers enrolling on courses. Many students who were awarded their B.Sc. in Computing Science from Griffith College during this time subsequently became successful entrepreneurs and were in a position to take advantage of the momentous growth in the software industry. Significant numbers of students also came from Northern Ireland to study at Griffith College, as grant aid from the British government made this possible. Tomás remarked that, "Diarmuid is a charismatic businessman who allows people the opportunity to develop an idea. He doesn't stop thinking about new ideas just because it is 5 p.m. and he expects the team around him to do the same. I have learned a lot from working with him and he is a terrific role model for all of us".

Two issues however, were to halt the growth and challenge the success of Griffith College in the mid 1990s. Firstly, in 1995 the "Rainbow" government, a combination of the Labour Party, Democratic Left (since merged with the Labour Party) and Fine Gael, decided to remove tertiary fees for Irish and EU students engaged in their first primary degree. This decision came into effect in January 1996. As Griffith College was competing directly with the State, free third level education in State-funded third level colleges seemed to pose an insurmountable challenge. Why would anyone choose to pay for their education when it was available free from State universities and colleges?

Secondly, in 1996 Michael Anchram of the British government withdrew funding for Northern Irish students to study in the Republic, thus drying up a major source of revenue. In order to survive these years the company had to think creatively and come up with innovative solutions. Business Studies, Journalism, Design, Business and Law were added to the college's prospectus as the board decided that these were the most cost-effective faculties to run. It also started to pursue overseas markets to fill the gap left by Northern Irish students. Diarmuid recalls:

> We made a conscious decision that we were going to move into undergraduate level provision and expand that area. I guess that, in terms of the validation, quality assurance and registration, Tomás was the key person.

IDENTIFYING NEW OPPORTUNITIES

One major advantage that Griffith had was that, as a result of poor planning by the Department of Education, there was under-provision of third level courses by State-funded colleges, and demand exceeded supply. In the 1980s if Irish students did not receive their first preference within the Central Applications Office (CAO) system, many were forced to travel to the UK where they could undertake the course of their choice. This, coupled with the fact that Griffith did not have to adhere to CAO guidelines, ensured that students who met the course verifiers' minimum entry requirements could be accepted onto their chosen course. Diarmuid was confident that the college would expand rapidly if it were to fill this gap in the market:

> I felt there was a real market for third level qualifications. I could see so many not getting their career or education path within the public sector at that time so I could see there was clearly a need. I knew somebody would fill it and I remember consciously in the late 80s and early 90s saying that I would be kicking myself having worked at that stage for fifteen years full-time, having built up the team and built up the organisation, if we hadn't brought it to the third level arena.

The company's expansion continued, with the Lenister School of Music and Drama joining GCD. Students past and present are prominent performers both at national and international level, with some appearing at the National Concert Hall, as well as other venues throughout Ireland, and others employed by orchestras and opera companies around the globe. Newman College, a private college located in Dublin's city centre, was taken over by Griffith College in the late 1990s.

Despite the challenges it had encountered, Griffith College faces the new millennium with enthusiasm and a strong sense of purpose. Student numbers continue to increase, new faculties and facilities are being developed and the college is recognised today as an important player in Irish third level education. In the last two years, three professional accountancy students achieved a first in the world examinations, and first in ACCA examinations in Ireland (see Exhibits 3 and 4). In 2004,[6] Griffith became the first independent college in the country to have its degrees (LL.B. and B.A. in Business & Law) accredited by the Honorable Society of King's Inns. This means that graduates of these programmes have direct access to the King's Inns' entrance examinations without having to first complete the Inns' diploma course or qualifying diploma examinations. All degree programmes offered by the college are validated by the Higher Education and Training Awards Council (HETAC) or Nottingham Trent University (NTU). Students can apply for many courses at the college using the CAO application system. They also have the option of applying directly to the college. In 2004 halls of residence opened accommodating both national and international students. The campus in Karachi, which started to deliver courses in 1999, is winding down its operations, and Moscow, which opened in February 2003, still remains a challenge for the college and has yet to show a profit. Griffith recently won a two-year contract with the accountancy company KPMG to train its staff in professional accountancy in Russia.

STRATEGIC LEADERSHIP, DEVELOPMENT AND PLANNING

Diarmuid is conscious of the role strategic planning and development plays in the continued growth of the company. He and his Board of Directors have identified a number of key areas for the future:

- further international expansion
- more academic centres
- the promotion of academic research
- the development of partnerships within industry

The reasons that these targets have been identified and the particular corporate or strategic goals they will achieve have not yet been clearly articulated. Diarmuid is all too aware that some strategic planning should have taken place earlier:

> The markets have worked out well for us but we could have perhaps started to "export" earlier. There are markets we have not yet exploited and have yet to develop; for example, one market we have not yet explored is North America, but that is something we are conscious of and have been working on for the last two years.

Griffith College employs in excess of 400 members of staff but does not have formal documented human resource policies or a strategic approach to human resource management. In fact, no Board member has responsibility for HRM. It could, in fact, be argued that the company does not have a coherent approach to human resource management at all. Many of the academic staff are employed on part-time contracts, which raises questions about commitment and loyalty. If decisions about the employees of an organisation are not aligned with its overall strategic planning, then the company is unable to ensure that its human resources contribute to accomplishment of its mission and that managers are held accountable for human resource decisions. It can also lead to other problems in the workplace: for example, staff morale may fall and employees may feel that their contribution to the overall success of the organisation is not valued. Diarmuid is fully aware of this:

> I think there are always going to be gaps. What you tend to do is double jobbing – I guess we have done that very successfully over the years. Then, as a particular role grew, we tended to look for somebody to fill it. What you need is a fairly flexible and widely skilled team that can fill a gap, develop the role and then pass it on to somebody. But I also see the staff at Griffith as a community; they are all working to achieve a common goal.

While Diarmuid may enjoy the fact that he knows most of the staff personally, the need for a formal structure may be more important. In fact, at the time of writing, a position for a Senior Human Resource Manager had just been created.

In January 2005, the Minister for Education and Science, Mary Hanafin, led a delegation of over forty senior representatives of universities, institutes of technology, independent colleges – including Griffith College – and language schools as part of the largest-ever Irish trade mission to China. The aim of this joint session was to promote links between Irish and Chinese third level institutes and to promote Ireland as a destination for Chinese students seeking to study abroad. A number of bilateral agreements between individual Irish education institutions and partner Chinese institutions were signed during the visit. As a result, Griffith College set up an office in Beijing. Diarmuid Hegarty was also part of the Taoiseach's trade mission to India in 2006. While it is evident that GCD is taking advantage of the international expansion opportunities that are presented to it, it is not clear how this strategy fits with the more formal strategic planning and structure that needs to be in place.

MARKETING MANAGEMENT

Education in Ireland is highly competitive. Not only does Griffith College compete with State-funded colleges throughout the country, but there are also a number of other private third level colleges.[7]

Diarmuid estimates that Griffith spends in excess of €1.2 million on both national and international marketing each year. This includes international education trade fairs and exhibitions. Marketing from a national perspective includes visits to secondary schools throughout the country, open days, and the company's advertisement on the Setanta television channel during the inter-schools rugby championships. Griffith also advertises on the local and national media throughout Ireland. All of this marketing is supported by a new modern website.

Diarmuid feels that marketing is also a weakness of the college:

> Our marketing activities are not audited and, therefore, it
> is difficult to assess value for money. We have also iden-
> tified that brand awareness and brand building by the col-
> lege is poor. There is plenty of evidence that customers
> will pay a substantial price premium for a good brand and

remain loyal to that brand. What we have not yet identified is when a potential student hears the name Griffith College, what brand image enters his or her head? Brand building needs to become a priority for the college.

Perhaps an overall brand for the college could be developed or, alternatively, each faculty could attempt to develop a brand that it markets to its potential students. At the moment there is no local, national or international marketing plan or, indeed, a marketing strategy in place and, should competitors adopt a more aggressive marketing strategy, Griffith's future could be jeopardized. However, as Diarmuid points out, there is nothing certain in education:

> We must ensure that we deliver what the customers want and we must ensure that potential customers, both national and international, know the courses we offer and that we offer an excellent learning environment where meeting the students' needs is paramount to the college's success.

MOVING FORWARD – THE CHALLENGES AHEAD

Although Griffith College was initially established to meet the third level educational needs of Irish accounting students, it has quickly developed into an international provider of a wide range of courses. Even though there were a number of hurdles, under Diarmuid's leadership the college is now very successful. However, if the Chairman, the Board of Directors and the management team had been more strategically focused at an earlier stage, Griffith may now have a greater share of the market. As a result of a lack of strategic focus, the company has potentially missed out on some key opportunities. How will the company make decisions regarding managing growth, changes in the marketplace and the exploitation of new opportunities? Diarmuid feels that he has a strong management team in place and that together with his colleagues he has brought Griffith onto solid ground. However, he is also fully aware that more international opportunities exist and there is also the possibility of developing new academic areas, such as medicine, that can be sold to the national and international markets.

Diarmuid Hegarty – Griffith College Dublin

As Diarmuid goes into the Board meeting he realizes that the company must now develop a realistic corporate strategy for the future to ensure its survival in the highly competitive market in which it operates. This strategy will need to address long-term goals and objectives, including those relating to human resources, international expansion, marketing and diversity within the management structure. Like it or not, the issue of succession planning will have to be dealt with at some point. While Diarmuid's original entrepreneurial vision needs to be reflected in Griffith's future strategy, the company is only too aware that at some stage it will be moving forward with a new leader at the helm.

NOTES

1   This case was prepared by Geraldine McGing and Dr Pauline Connolly as the basis for class discussion rather than to illustrate either effective or ineffective handling of a business situation.

2   The authors are extremely grateful to Diarmuid Hegarty and the other directors and staff in GCD for their time and inspiration in helping to prepare this case, Geraldine McGing lectures at Griffith College Dublin and Pauline Connolly lectures at the Institute of Public Administration (Geraldine.Mcging@gcd.ie; p.connolly@ipa.ie).

3   Interview with Diarmuid Hegarty, 4 September 2006. All other quotations from Diaramuid Hegarty are from the same interview.

4   Interview with Reg Callanan, 4 December 2006.

5   Interview with Tomás MacEochagain, 20 September 2006.

6   Interview with Philip Bourke, 20 September 2006.

7   Interview with Ronan Fenlon, 2 November 2006.

Exhibit 1
Chairman of Griffith College, Diarmuid Hegarty

Exhibit 2
Griffith College Campus Map

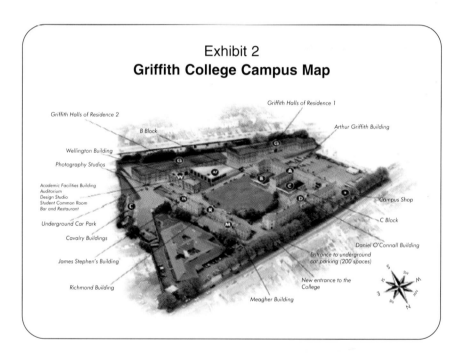

Exhibit 3
Griffith Awards – First & Third in World

The School of Professional Accountancy is the leading Irish educator of past and future accountants. The school has numerous prize-winners with all of the main accountancy bodies in Ireland. ACCA Paper 3.2 Stephen Gahan and James Bradley – 1st and 3rd in the World June 2006.

Exhibit 4
Griffith Awards – First in ACCA Finals

The School of Professional Accountancy at Griffith College: First in Ireland ACCA finals June 2005

Christopher Watson Chain Reaction Cycles[1]

Sharon Porter[2]

Introduction

It is another busy morning of commercial intrigue for Chris Watson, Director of Chain Reaction Cycles – Europe's largest e-based retailer of mountain bikes, bike parts, and related clothing and footwear. From trouble-shooting a courier to ensure that customer orders are delivered on time for Christmas, through to dealing with the multinational giant Goggle, with whom it is launching a new advertising campaign. In addition, Chris and his team have also unearthed a cutthroat attack from a competitor who has been using dirty tricks to undermine their business by bombarding their website with hits – no doubt an attempt to overwhelm their online system through a huge increase in traffic. Fortunately, the team were able to track and block the source of the traffic through a specialist software pro-gramme they developed. This is just one in a series of operational chal-lenges that the business continues to face in its efforts to consolidate its market position. From a strategic perspective, plans are already in place to extend its current premises, which will inevitably mean further invest-ment. Future challenges also include developing a call centre to support its global market, and ensuring the right team is in place to move the busi-ness forward. Despite its quiet backwater location, life is certainly not boring at Chain Reaction Cycles.

Company Background

Chris's parents, Janice and George Watson, originally established their retail cycling business in 1984. Seed capital for the start-up was derived

143

from a STG£1,500 redundancy payment. Then called Ballynure Cycles, it was based in the town of Ballynure, outside Ballyclare, Co. Antrim. Chris was involved in the family business from an early age. He also started to develop a keen interest in mountain biking and started competing in his late teens at a local level. An enthusiast at the sport of mountain biking, his organisational skills were developed in the process of dealing with local government bodies to arrange and promote cycle events.

After completing a BTEC National Diploma in Computer Studies, Chris embarked on a degree in Computer Science at the University of Ulster, Jordanstown. After two years of study and a work placement, Chris decided this was not the route for him and that he wanted to focus all of his energy on developing the family business. He had a vision to take their local bike-selling outlet to a national level and beyond.

The Development of Chain Reaction Cycles

In 1990 the business moved to a main street store in Ballyclare and was renamed Chain Reaction Cycles. At this point, the company began to offer a mail order service to expand the business beyond the needs of the local market. Employee levels grew from two to five over this period. Around this time, Chris began to manage the business and succeeded in negotiating his first big deal, an advertising campaign in a specialist magazine for a rock bottom fee of STG£100 (the starting price had been STG£300!).

1996 saw Chain Reaction Cycles outgrow its main street retail premises. A tough decision was needed: move to a larger high street retail store and establish the business firmly in the local market, or expand the mail order side considerably by moving to an industrial warehouse unit, a decision that could effectively kill off its retail potential. It decided to forego the retail aspect and move to a 1,800 square foot industrial unit in Avondale Business Park. Employee levels grew from five to eight over this period.

The business became a limited company in 1999. The mail order service was expanded to a web-based ordering service using the domain name <http://www.chainreactioncycles.com> (see Exhibits 1 and 2). Chain Reaction Cycles underwent rapid expansion, which saw the business utilising five separate units totalling 12,500 square feet. This split operation, although still within the business park, put extensive pressure on the company and, as a result, growth became difficult to manage. For example, stock location and management, technical infrastructure and efficiency were all much more costly and time consuming to manage. This resulted in an ever-increasing slip in customer service levels, which in turn, restricted company growth.

In addition, between 1999 and early 2003 employment levels grew to forty. It became very clear that a single outlet was required which could facilitate the rapid growth that the business was experiencing. However, this was not an easy task, and several options were explored. A site was finally found in late 2004 at Kilbride. The building was completed in July 2005 and greatly facilitated the further expansion of the business, which now accommodates 100 employees (see Exhibits 3 and 4). Its location, in close proximity to the Royal Mail at Mallusk and the DHL Office at Belfast International Airport, has been beneficial for distribution purposes and has helped to keep operational costs to a minimum. The outdoor image associated with the business was also helped by the semi-rural move, which was considered a bonus by many of the company's stakeholders and helped to reinforce the positive environmental perception of the business.

Chain Reaction Cycles enjoy a longstanding relationship with the local community, and it has been estimated that it contributes around STG£1 million to the local economy in wages and salaries each year. It is the largest employer in the Ballyclare area. In July 2006, to facilitate further growth, plans were submitted for an extension at Kilbride. The additional space created will accommodate a forecasted growth in employee numbers to 150 over the next 6–18 months.

Product Range

While Chain Reaction Cycles is essentially an e-based retailer of mountain bikes, mountain bike parts, and related clothing and footwear, the business is currently diversifying by offering associated products such as snowboarding equipment, motor cross equipment, and enthusiast radio-controlled toys. The company also has plans to develop its branded product range further to facilitate cross-selling to a wider market. In addition, Chris, in partnership with two other sales managers, has also started a wholesale distribution business targeted at the UK and Irish markets. This part of the business trades under a different name.

INDUSTRY BACKGROUND

From 2000, factors such as foot-and-mouth disease, terrorist attacks, bad weather and economic uncertainty contributed to a deflation in consumer bike-related spending within the UK, European and the US markets. Indeed, as in many sectors, 2001 was considered the 'annus horriblis' for the industry. Many leading players in the industry, for example Schinn/GT and Derby Cycles, went out of business, while others blossomed as a result of their demise.[3]

While accurate statistics are difficult to obtain for the bike industry, it is estimated that in 2000 the UK market declined by approximately 30 per cent and in 2001 the European market declined by 15–20 per cent.[4] However, things began to improve from 2003/2004 onwards due to a number of factors, including the following:

• Cycling promotion initiatives:

The Bike Hub Scheme was launched by the UK bike industry to promote bicycle usage and expand the market through a levy fund. More recently, British Cycling also set up the Everyday Cycling programme, which challenges national recreational cyclists to cycle one million miles in 2007. The online portal <http://www.everydaycycling.com> provides an activity log, events and useful information to encourage greater participation and, in its first three months, the site attracted an additional 2,676 registered users.[5] National carbon neutrality targets, along with an increasing recognition that most of us should be using our bikes rather than our cars for short urban journeys, have also strengthened the cycling lobby, particularly with the introduction of a congestion charge in London, and the threat of such measures in other areas. For example, for the period from May 2000 to May 2005, cycle journeys in London increased from 60,000 to over 100,000.[6]

• The obesity crisis:

As a result of an increasing sedentary lifestyle, obesity is reported to cost the National Health Service STG£7.5 billion per year, with three-quarters of the adult UK population now considered overweight or obese. According to Bikebiz, obesity levels have grown faster in England than in any other European country, with child obesity levels tripling in the last twenty years.[7] In its strategy to deal with this crisis, the Government has highlighted cycling as a key component in encouraging the British public to get fitter and shed the pounds, and has developed the National Cycling Strategy. The British Government has set a target to treble cycling participation between 2000 and 2010.

- Improved weather and infrastructure:

  Be it global warning or not, we have enjoyed some glorious cycling weather over recent summers which has greatly helped to boost general participation levels, bike sales and cycling tourism. In addition, recent years have seen a substantial increase in funding provision for cycle-friendly infrastructure in our towns and cities, as well as the development of off-road routes and mountain bike parks. For example, the 2005 International Mountain Bicycling Association (IMBA) Report Card awarded Scotland an 'A' for "outstanding mountain biking and successful bicycle advocacy", beating British Columbia. The potential gain for Scottish cycling tourism, and the mountain biking sector overall, of such international promotion is priceless, and very good news, of course, for prominent specialist retailers like Chain Reaction Cycles.

- Increased terrorism threat:

  Such world events as the 7 July attacks in London in 2005, which crippled the city's transportation system, have also inadvertently helped to boost cycling journeys. The benefits of cycling as a mode of commuting became clear as car traffic sat gridlocked. Evans Cycles reported a four-fold increase in bike sales that day and later that year the Mayor of London, Ken Livingstone, reported that 650,000 Londoners cycle on a daily basis.[8]

THE MARKET

The world market for bicycles, parts and accessories is estimated to be worth $20 billion, with approximately 100 million bicycles being produced per year.[9] The UK bicycle market is worth approximately STG£500 million per year.[10] In 2004, 4.5 million bicycles were sold in the UK.[11] According to British Cycling, over 2 million bikes are sold in the UK each year.[12]

The global marketplace is dominated by a small number of big players such as Trek and Giant. Trek, for example, had a turnover of $375 million in 2001, while Giant turned over $425 million in 2000.[13] In 2004, 144 bicycle brands existed in Europe while, for the same period, only 66 existed in the US.[14]

The main UK bike retailer is Halfords who, as Exhibit 5 highlights, also currently have the most visited UK sport and fitness website, with a 4.2 per cent share of the sport and fitness market. As Halfords not only sell bicycles, it is interesting to note Chain Reactions Cycles' position of number 6 in the market, with a 1.58 per cent share, one which is largely cycling-related. Other prominent retailers include Edinburgh Bicycle (Scotland's largest bike retailer).

Bikebiz predict that the demand for bikes will increase over the next ten years in the UK. This will be partly due to the work of the National Cycle Network and the many government-sponsored, cycle-friendly initiatives that exist. However, Bikebiz also warn that the multiplicity of brands, and the high number of independent cycle retailers, will make for a potentially crowded and highly competitive marketplace.

It would appear that the grey market will be a key market as the population ages. In its report on the European Sports Goods Market[15] (January 2001), the Sporting Goods Manufacturers Association forecasted:

> With the ageing population and consequent increase in leisure time and travel, the emphasis in sports participation will be less on the competitive team sports and more on leisure and individual sports. This development will stimulate the market for outdoor activities (footwear, clothing, rucksacks), golf equipment, fitness goods (in-home trainers, fitness clothing), water sports and snow sports equipment. On the other hand, young people will favour adventurous, alternative, beach, fun and extreme sports.

MARKETING STRATEGY

With a worldwide customer base of over 300,000, Chain Reaction Cycles ships approximately 25,000–30,000 packages per month. At present, the

UK mainland accounts for 65 per cent of sales, while other EU countries contribute 20 per cent, with the rest of the world accounting for 10 per cent, and Ireland 5 per cent.

Chain Reaction Cycles' success can be attributed to the following key elements:

- E-commerce strategy: an early recognition of the contribution the Internet could make in helping it to become a global player was a major turning point for the company, and it quickly set about harnessing the power of the Internet to do just that. It teamed up with Belfast-based company Export Technologies to develop and maintain a website that would enable it to develop a professional online retail presence. In 2004, it began to lead the market. Today, 80 per cent of orders are via web-based sales, while telesales account for 18 per cent and the showroom 2 per cent of sales. Its award-winning website is translated into four languages, reflecting its global focus.

- Market knowledge: Chain Reaction Cycles knows its market very well. Chris's personal interest in biking has greatly contributed to this, as well as his involvement with the family business from a young age. The team, which he has since build around him, has helped to sustain this leading edge.

- Competitor knowledge: Chain Reaction Cycles has spent a lot of time and energy assessing its competition, developing its own competitive advantage and then challenging them head-on.

- Customer focus: Chris and his team have worked hard to exceed the expectations of their customer base. It is now Europe's largest online bike store, delivering an exacting customer service level which, for example, promises a free next day delivery service to anywhere in the UK or Ireland. Providing a first rate customer care programme has also been a clear focus of its recruitment process. For example, tele-sales team members include an Elite XC and Road racer, an Elite DH racer, an expert UK Trials rider and two avid Free Riders, while the head mechanic is an Elite DH rider. This has provided the company with over fifteen years experience in the UK mountain bike scene. Chain Reaction Cycles' level of attention and customer care has been acknowledged not only in its sales figures but also in the number of awards and accolades it has received. In 2006 it was winner of the

'Specialist On-Line Retailer of the Year Award' at the Irish Outdoor Adventure Awards.

- A loyal customer base: the company enjoys a high level of repeat business and very positive word-of-mouth promotion. Customers are willing to pay a premium for the high level of customer service associated with the company.

- Focused promotional campaigns: Chain Reaction Cycles' customer service philosophy is communicated through its advertising strap lines: "Europe's largest online bike store" and "free next day delivery". They form a core feature of its advertising campaigns, which are not purely Internet-based, but also promoted via the specialist press, shows and events. For example, in 2007 the company are main sponsors of TransScotland '07, a seven-day mountain bike stage event, and the first ever National Bike Show. It has also been associated with the British Cycling National Downhill Series. As a result of such focused activity it has established a distinct online presence in a marketplace that is growing day-by-day.

CUSTOMER SERVICE AND DISTRIBUTION

Chain Reaction Cycles prides itself on offering a free next day delivery service to anywhere in the UK and Ireland. But how can it achieve this? It is all down to providing a exacting customer service based on precision, working hand-in-hand with its courier providers and developing high-tech solutions to ensure it can meet its promise. For example, orders received before 4 p.m. are processed, picked, packed and, depending on destination, dispatched via one of three courier companies used by the business: the Royal Mail, Parcel Force or DHL. This process takes between 20 and 60 minutes.

All orders are downloaded from the website onto an in-house-designed and custom-written computer system. Orders are then checked for fraud, credit cards are processed and orders are dispatched to the store for picking. The relevant stock is selected for the order and passed to the dispatch area for checking and packing. The order is packed and dispatched again through the use of a custom-written integrated software system and bagged, ready for collection by the courier. Couriers arrive between 4 p.m. and 5 p.m. to load their vans. Loading is completed between 5 p.m. and 5.45 p.m., and the couriers depart either for direct DHL aircraft loading at Belfast International Airport, or for onward transportation by the Royal Mail at Mallusk. This relationship has taken years to develop and has been facilitated through the use of technology that allows Chain Reaction Cycles to bypass most of the sorting procedures employed by the couriers, thus enabling it to deliver its products direct from the warehouse to the customer. The company currently ships to over 100 countries worldwide, supplying products from more than 300 brands direct to the end consumer. Products are sourced from all over the world and via distributors in Ireland, Northern Ireland, the UK, Europe and the Far East. Stock largely arrives in bulk and is either repackaged or finished ready for sale. They are then entered for sale via the website.

CHRIS – THE ENTREPRENEUR

Chris, by his own admission, is very opportunity-focused and driven. He has a passion for what he does and a great personal interest in biking. Part of Chain Reaction Cycles' success can be attributed to Chris's analytical mindset and innovative problem-solving approach. This has been demonstrated by how the company has been able to identify and exploit the benefits of online retailing by combining extensive market knowledge with cutting-edge technology. He is also very aware of the potential global market place and its vast potential, potential that he and his team are not afraid of pursuing.

Despite having no formal enterprise training, Chris has natural business acumen. He has also been gifted with an entrepreneurial spirit, which has helped to drive the business success that the company has so far enjoyed. He is a calculated risk-taker who weights up the pros and cons, and always considers the feasibility of the opportunities presented to him, or as Chris puts it: "it's important to know what to focus on and to not spread yourself too thin".[16]

In conversation with Chris it is very clear that his father has been a very influential role model.

> My father did what he could to survive and is a very resourceful person. His influence helped to shape my own work ethic and determination to succeed.

Chris's IT background has also been of real benefit to the development of the company, as this gave him a technical insight into how to fully exploit the benefits of e-commerce and to develop IT solutions that would improve operational efficiency. As well as using external expertise in the early days, it has since developed the in-house capability and infrastructure required to secure and maintain the title of "Europe's largest online bike store".

Chain Reaction Cycles reviews its business plan on a regular basis as the market is constantly evolving and growing. As Chris points out, "there has been a lot of learning and we have had a very steep learning curve".

KEY CHALLENGES

In its development to date, Chain Reaction Cycles has faced a number of challenges, most of which relate to the growth and management of the business. In terms of growth, the main challenges can be summarised as follows:

- Securing funding: a privately owned company, all developments to date have been funded without government support. Thus, the full financial risk has been born by the proprietors of the company.
- Building the right team: Chris has headhunted core team members over the years and has focused on building an effective and committed team around him. He attributes the success of Chain Reaction Cycles to his staff.
- Obtaining sufficient accommodation: securing the appropriate space to facilitate the growth required to enable the company to achieve its full potential. This continues to be an issue for Chain Reaction Cycles as it attempts to progress its current expansion plans in the face of Belfast-centric bureaucracy, which is putting pressure on the company to relocate to Belfast: a move that would be contrary to the interests of Chain Reaction Cycles and its stakeholders.

With regard to management, Chris has had to deal with the twin challenges of managing a growing company and making the transitition from a small family business to a much larger organisation. This has involved moving from a very informal working environment to one which is becoming increasingly more structured as the company grows. Chris emphasises that while a more structured approach is required it is also important that staff consider Chain Reaction Cycles as a fun place to work.

As Chris points out, "the challenge is to keep a handle on what is happening". Part of his approach involves him spending a lot of time with his team in order to get the best from them by utilising their key strengths and abilities. Part of his personal progression has been to learn how to delegate: "I've had to learn to let go". Not an easy task for someone who has been so hands-on for so long.

THE FUTURE

While Chain Reaction Cycles are now recognised as the premier online retail brand in the marketplace, it is seeking to use its position to make further inroads into markets that it has not yet sufficiently penetrated, such as Germany and the Far East. It plans to develop a call centre to help facilitate the continued expansion of its global market. If its strategy is successful, it will propel the company into a new stratosphere of operation with a significant increase in turnover. Plans are already in progress to extend the current premises, and this may also mean significant further investment, a new recruitment drive and an international marketing campaign. But is it up to the challenge?

When Chris first joined the family business, he had a vision to take its local retail outlet to a national level and beyond. Now, with a customer base of over 300,000 located in over 100 countries, Chris has certainly achieved his initial objective. To turn a small family business into "Europe's largest online bike store" is a major achievement and clearly demonstrates Chris's commitment and drive. Despite having some tough up-hill challenges, Chain Reaction Cycles appears set to enjoy some "free-wheeling on the down-hills" as it moves into the future.

NOTES

1   This case was prepared by Sharon Porter as the basis for class discussion rather than to illustrate either effective or ineffective handling of a business situation.

2   Sharon Porter is a lecturer in Entrepreneurship with the Northern Ireland Centre for Entrepreneurship, University of Ulster (s.porter@ulster.ac.uk). The author is extremely grateful to Chris Watson for his time and inspiration in helping to prepare this case.

3   <http://www.bikebiz.co.uk>

4   <http://www.bike-eu.com>, November 2001

5   British Cycling (2006) *Annual Report.*

6   <http://www.bikebiz.co.uk>

7   <http://www.bikebiz.co.uk>

8   <http://www.bikebiz.co.uk>

9   Derby Cycle Corporation (April 2001) *Annual Accounts*, p. 18.

10   CTC/Bicycle Association/Association of Cycle Traders (April 2001) Press Release.

11   Bicycle Association of Great Britain, 2004

12   British Cycling (2006) *Annual Report*, p. 24.

13   *Bicycle Business*, 2001, pp. 23–24.

14   *The B.O.S.S. Report*, June 2004

15   Sporting Goods Manufacturers Association (January 2001), 'The European Sports Goods Market'.

16   Interview with Chris Watson on 13 December 2006. All other quotations from Chris Watson are from the same interview.

Exhibit 1
Screen-shot from www.chainreactioncycles.com

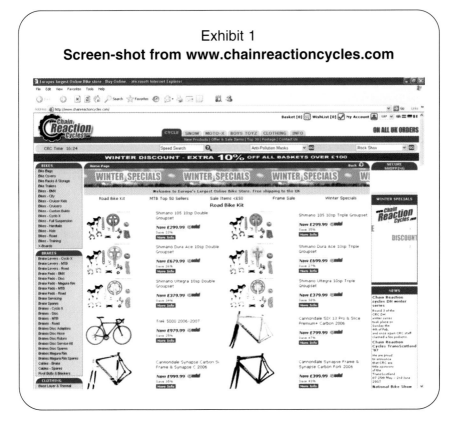

Exhibit 2
Screen-shot from www.chainreactioncycles.com

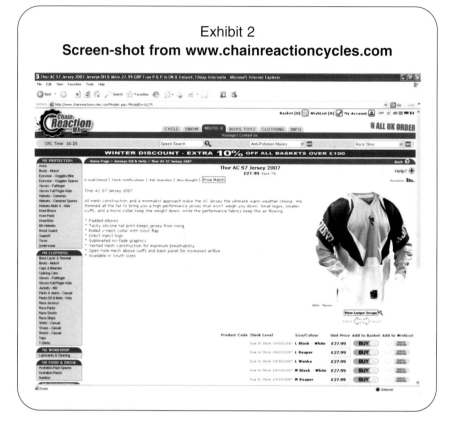

Exhibit 3
External view of the premises of Chain Reaction Cycles

Exhibit 4
**Internal view of the premises of Chain Reaction
Cycles – Warehousing**

Exhibit 5
Top 10 most visited UK Sport and Fitness websites*

	Site	Market Share (%)
1	www.halfords.com	4.2
2	www.mandmdirect.com	3.9
3	www.jjbsports.com	3.06
4	www.jdsports.co.uk	2.93
5	www.wiggle.co.uk	1.99
6	www.chainreactioncycles.com	1.58
7	www.predirectsoccer.com	1.57
8	www.kitbag.com	1.51
9	www.direct-golf.co.uk	1.28
10	www.millets.co.uk	1.23

*Figures for week to 10 March 2007 (*Source*: *Retail Week*, March 2007).